Dear Blake,

I think this
reminder on the

good.

THE ETF STRATEGIST

THE **ETF**
STRATEGIST

BALANCING RISK AND REWARD
FOR SUPERIOR RETURNS

Russ Koesterich

PORTFOLIO

PORTFOLIO
Published by the Penguin Group
Penguin Group (USA) Inc., 375 Hudson Street, New York, New York 10014, U.S.A. •
Penguin Group (Canada), 90 Eglinton Avenue East, Suite 700, Toronto, Ontario, Canada
M4P 2Y3 (a division of Pearson Penguin Canada Inc.) • Penguin Books Ltd, 80 Strand,
London WC2R 0RL, England • Penguin Ireland, 25 St. Stephen's Green, Dublin 2, Ireland
(a division of Penguin Books Ltd) • Penguin Books Australia Ltd, 250 Camberwell Road,
Camberwell, Victoria 3124, Australia (a division of Pearson Australia Group Pty Ltd) •
Penguin Books India Pvt Ltd, 11 Community Centre, Panchsheel Park, New Delhi – 110
017, India • Penguin Group (NZ), 67 Apollo Drive, Rosedale, North Shore 0632, New
Zealand (a division of Pearson New Zealand Ltd) • Penguin Books (South Africa) (Pty)
Ltd, 24 Sturdee Avenue, Rosebank, Johannesburg 2196, South Africa

Penguin Books Ltd, Registered Offices:
80 Strand, London WC2R 0RL, England

First published in 2008 by Portfolio,
a member of Penguin Group (USA) Inc.

10   9   8   7   6   5   4   3   2   1

Publisher's Note
This publication is designed to provide accurate and authoritative information in regard to
the subject matter covered. It is sold with the understanding that the publisher is not engaged
in rendering legal, accounting or other professional services. If you require legal advice or
other expert assistance, you should seek the services of a competent professional.

Library of Congress Cataloging-in-Publication Data
Koesterich, Russ.
The ETF strategist : balancing risk and reward for superior returns / Russ Koesterich.
       p.   cm.
Includes bibliographical references and index.
ISBN-13: 978-1-59184-207-1
1. Exchange traded funds. I. Title.
HG6043.K64 2008
332.63'27—dc22   2007040173

Printed in the United States of America
Set in Minion with Eurostyle
Designed by Daniel Lagin

CONTENTS

INTRODUCTION

Investors often look to financial books with the same dogged hope that those looking to lose weight place in diet books. And just as no diet, no matter how elaborate or simple, can reverse the simple truism of eating less and getting more exercise, no financial book can ease the basic reality of financial security: save more and spend less. Fad diets rarely result in prolonged weight loss, and rarely will a new technique or financial gimmick unilaterally enhance your financial well-being. Finance is as susceptible to fashions and fads as any other industry, although often at a considerably higher cost. A cursory look at the last several decades reveals several products that have come and gone, sometimes leaving more than a bit of financial wreckage in their wake.

So a book dedicated to a new, or at least trendy, financial innovation should be greeted with the same skepticism as late-night advertisements for diamond-hard abs or self-cleaning kitchen whisks. Financial security, like physical fitness, comes with few shortcuts— old and dull admonitions like "save more" are as relevant today as when they were first issued. But once an investor has developed the basic discipline to adopt a regular savings plan, what then? He or she is still left with a barrage of choices and competing advice, much of it contradictory. Should you overweight stocks, or bonds? Invest, or trade? And what about international versus domestic investing? (If you are already looking to skip ahead to the conclusion, the correct answers are [1] stocks *and* bonds; [2] invest, don't trade; and [3] international *and* domestic, although more international.)

Choices are a good thing, but the human mind quickly becomes overwhelmed when bombarded by a virtually limitless set of options. As when facing a menu at a New Jersey diner, which can easily clock in at more than a hundred entrees, at some point it is just easier to give in and order the same old thing. And like that at the diner, the menu of financial products has exploded over the past decade. Adding to the confusion, defined benefit pension plans are in decline, and most individuals in their twenties and thirties are justifiably skeptical about their prospects of ever seeing a Social Security check. Finally, for investors who grew of age during the eighties or nineties, the last six or seven years have seemed less forgiving by comparison. While international and small-cap stocks have done well, large-capitalization U.S. stocks have taken seven years to eclipse their 2000 peak. And while the broader market has recovered, for those individuals unfortunate enough to buy into technology stocks at their peak, the 1990s seem like another age. Tech stocks, the darlings of the last decade, have never regained their former glamour, with the NASDAQ market still languishing at barely 50 percent of its 2000 high. Taken in aggregate, it is not hard to see why most Americans admit to a significant amount of financial insecurity, despite a good labor market and a generally strong economy.

So the challenges facing individual investors are several: too many products, most of which are inappropriate for ordinary investors; lower equity returns; and the erosion of the corporate and government safety net. The good news is that in many respects, it is now both easier and cheaper for individuals to invest than at any time in history. While markets are just as capricious and volatile as they have always been, investors can now access choices that did not exist until recently. For example, international investing is now much easier and cheaper than in the past. As solid financial portfolios are based on diversity, having access to new markets is no trivial thing. Investors also face considerably lower transaction costs (the price of buying and selling shares and bonds, or securities) than they have ever had. So while the basic principals of building a sound portfolio have remained the same—save, diversify, and keep costs down— following the last two truisms has become a bit simpler.

In a broad sense, this book is about these last two principles: diversification and controlling the costs of investing. While neither is very sexy or exciting, they form the basis of a sound investment philosophy. Everyone dreams of the stock that will make them rich, but real-world investing means first concentrating on the basics. The investor who can only focus on finding the next Google is no different from the high school basketball player who wants to take shots from the half-court line before first developing a consistent free throw. Most investors would be surprised at how much they can improve their performance by just focusing on these basics. Paying attention to costs will help remove the drag on returns caused by overpriced financial products and services, while diversification will reduce excess volatility in your portfolio. Now, as stated above, achieving these objectives has become a bit simpler. In particular, the evolution of exchange traded funds, or ETFs, has given individual investors access to new markets, in a simple product, and at a cheaper cost.

What is unique about the exchange traded fund is that its principal benefit is not in raising returns, but in lowering risk. Risk management is a topic of serious concern for professional investors, but one that is often relegated to a footnote when discussing individual portfolios. Too many individuals have their gaze fixed on the stars, and are focused solely on the potential return of an investment with too little consideration for the accompanying risks. Yet, as most professional investors know, and as this book will illustrate, talking about returns without considering risk is a meaningless discussion. Returns are surprisingly easy to generate. Take more risk and over the long term you are likely to generate higher returns. The rub is that most investors are not indifferent to the level of risk in their portfolio. While everyone would like to enjoy greater than 20 percent annual returns, if made aware of the level of risk that would realistically be required to generate those returns, most investors would balk. The true metric of performance is how much return you can generate while constraining your risk to an acceptable level. This is how professionals measure their investment success, and it applies no less to individuals. In this context the exchange traded fund is a useful addition to most portfolios, specifically because it provides for greater precision in allocating risk.

The evolution of the ETF has occurred coincident to an explosion in the number and diversity of financial products. Over the past quarter century, new financial instruments have poured forth at a dizzying pace. Many of these instruments are known only by exotic labels that leave only the vaguest idea of what their true purpose is.

This category includes a gaggle of securities and derivatives with names like liquid yield option notes, collateralized bond obligations, inverse floaters, and mortgage-backed securities. Exchange traded funds represent one of these innovations, neither the most exotic nor the most recent. The first exchange traded funds were launched nearly twenty years ago on the Toronto Stock Exchange. However, while not the newest or most esoteric of the recent innovations, ETFs are quickly becoming one of the more popular. More important, their use is not limited to rocket scientists in hedge funds or the proprietary desks of major brokerage houses. The investors best situated to take advantage of these instruments are individuals and their investment advisers who are looking for a more efficient and elegant way to construct well-diversified portfolios.

Another characteristic differentiating this financial product from the others is its simplicity. Exchange traded funds are a vehicle for investing in a basket of financial instruments, traditionally stocks, but ETFs are increasingly extending to other asset classes such as bonds and commodities. The basket of assets normally mimics an index, which can be broad, such as the S&P 500, or narrowly defined, such as a collection of semiconductor stocks. Unlike derivatives, structured products, and other recent innovations, the value of an ETF is not dependent upon a complicated mathematical formula or financial model, but rather on the value of the underlying securities. In contrast, many of the instruments listed above were designed to facilitate more complicated and esoteric bets, many of which utilize some amount of borrowed money to magnify the returns on the investment. In this respect the ETF is unique in its applicability to the needs of retail, or individual, investors. In essence, the exchange traded fund is an improvement on an even older financial product, the mutual fund. The ETF captures the diversification benefits of the mutual fund and the cost benefits of an index fund, and combines them with real-time trading.

Soon after their introduction on the Toronto exchange, the American Stock Exchange launched the SPDR—an acronym for Standard & Poor's Depository Receipts—an ETF representing the popular S&P 500 stock index. That was followed by several new ETFs traded on the American Stock Exchange and the NASDAQ over-the-counter market. The ETF's real surge in popularity has been more recent, with most of the proliferation in products occurring over the past four or five years. As recently as the mid-nineties the number of exchange traded funds was only a few dozen. Since the turn of the decade that number has expanded exponentially, both domestically and internationally. According to a recent study by Morgan Stanley, the total value of exchange traded funds is approximately half a trillion dollars.[1] While this amount is still dwarfed by the size of the mutual fund market, it nevertheless marks an astonishing growth rate. The growth has been noticeable across two dimensions. First, the size of the market, measured by the assets under management (AUM), has mushroomed. Second, ETFs now cover a greater variety of asset classes. While once limited to equities, ETFs increasingly represent the entire spectrum of financial products. Since 2000, not only has the group expanded into new equity markets, but it has also branched out into other asset classes such as fixed-income and commodities.

This $500 billion-plus market in ETFs is spread out among hundreds of instruments, with more than 800 listings on more than 35 different exchanges, managed by 64 separate managers. Back in the 1990s there were only two or three different managers.[2] Recently the market has been expanding internationally, with much of the new growth occurring outside of the United States. The first half of 2006 witnessed a 30 percent surge in exchange traded funds overseas—twice the rate of growth in the United States. Indeed, during the same period, it was Singapore, Hong Kong, and Canada that experienced the largest percentage increases in assets under management. Judging by the number of sponsors who have recently filed for new funds, this rate of growth is expected to continue. The same Morgan Stanley report goes on to suggest that by 2011 the size of the market is expected to exceed $2 trillion.[3]

The recent growth in the size and diversity of the market suggests that the ETF has now reached a point of maturity where it can serve as the core of many different types of portfolios. From individual investors, to traditional mutual funds, to hedge funds, investors are relying on these instruments to make up an ever greater percentage of their overall portfolios. As the ETF expands into new markets and assets, this trend is likely to continue. Even five or six years ago the market for exchange traded funds was limited to stocks, or equities. Having a portfolio composed solely of ETFs would have been difficult given the lack of choices in other asset classes. As this restriction has abated with the launch of numerous fixed-income and commodity funds, it is now relatively easy to construct a portfolio made up exclusively of exchange traded funds.

As stated above, the primary benefits of using exchange traded funds include better diversification, risk control, and lower transaction costs. For this reason, this book will start with an examination of why these characteristics are so important for investors. Individual investors spend a good deal of their time focused on the potential return of an investment. While this book does not discourage investors from pursuing investments with high expected returns, it does go to some length to prove that return, without risk, is only half of the story. When thinking about risk, investors need to first consider the likely volatility of an investment, and then compare that risk to the expected return of the asset. Next, investors should evaluate their investments holistically, rather than in isolation. How does a particular stock or fund relate to the other assets in a portfolio? This is critical, as not all combinations of assets are equal. Some combinations are better than others. Certain stocks or funds complement each other, while others merely serve to increase the overall risk of your portfolio without necessarily contributing to the expected return. Omitting the issues of risk and diversification is like trying to cook a meal based only on the ingredients, with no thought about how to combine and cook them.

As these issues are central to the justification and benefit of exchange traded funds, the first part of the book examines them from different angles. It explores three themes: the prospect for lower market returns, the difficulty in isolating individual stocks that will beat the market, and the poor track record of professional money managers. What these themes have in common is that each, in its own way, constitutes a challenge for individual investors. Starting the discussion focused on the challenges in the market should make the ultimate rationale for a different investment approach much clearer.

All investors need to be aware of the difficulties of trying to beat the market through security selection. While this is the holy grail of both professional money managers and most individuals, it is an elusive goal. In an effort to address this challenge, chapter 2 explores the prospects of individual investors' trying to beat the market, through either security or manager selection. Trying to add value through stock picking, always a difficult proposition, has become even more challenging in the face of an increasingly better financed and more sophisticated professional investor.

Many individuals have already abandoned the quest for stocks that can produce outsized gains. For these investors, the answer has been to turn to the more sophisticated professional money manager and employ him or her to beat the market for them. Yet, as chapter 2 illustrates, while the professional money manager may be talented enough to produce modest excess returns ahead of the market, investors seldom share in those gains. For the most part, the active mutual fund industry has been better at generating fees than at producing excess returns for their investors.

In order to better confront these obstacles, investors may want to reconsider how they view their portfolio. One of the principal themes that will emerge from the first few chapters is the importance of thinking of your portfolio in terms of the risks it represents, rather than as simply a collection of stocks, bonds, and funds. Investors are conditioned to think of stocks as the basic building blocks of a portfolio, but if you take just one thing from this book, it should be to change your focus from stocks to risks. In order to provide a better understanding of what risk really means for financial assets, chapter 3 introduces some basic concepts of risk and return. The point of this digression is to help clarify the discussion and provide the necessary tool set for applying these concepts to exchange traded funds. The goal of this approach is to build portfolios that take into account not only what an asset may return, but also its inherent risks.

Chapter 3 borrows heavily from the field of quantitative finance in order to illustrate how to think about risk conceptually. This chapter also introduces another important concept, alpha/beta separation, which goes directly to the value proposition for exchange traded funds. This is a concept that is increasingly used in professional money management circles, but is potentially even more relevant for individual investors, as they are often the ones paying the largest fees. Despite the mathematical nomenclature, the concept of alpha/beta separation is remarkably simple. The idea states that returns from risk are not the same as returns generated by the skill of an active money manager. This ability to differentiate *alpha,* skill, from *beta,* risk, is critical in pricing financial products. While skill generally comes at a high price—a fund manager who can guarantee high returns can command high fees—risk should come cheap. Being able to separate the two will enable you to evaluate if the price you are paying for a financial service or product is related to the value being added.

Historically, investors have paid too little attention to disaggregating skill from pure risk taking. Higher returns have been greeted with joyful approbation, regardless of how those returns were generated. Yet without taking risk into account, it is impossible to know which part of your portfolio's return is coming from the skill of the manager, and which part is coming from sheer aggression. Aggressive managers will normally outperform in rising markets as their portfolios are simply more risky than those of more defensive managers. Yet taking on additional risk is something that every investor can easily replicate without the need to pay high fees for the privilege. Paying a professional money manager to take risks you can take on your own is no different from giving someone a few dollars to spin a roulette wheel for you. Most people are perfectly capable of spinning the wheel without paying someone else for the right.

Separating skill from risk becomes more nuanced, but just as important, when the risks the manager is taking are no longer related to the stock market in general but to a particular slice of it. If a money manager's whole approach is to leverage to one particular investment theme, exchange traded funds can accomplish the same thing for a fraction of the cost. Consider a fund manager who prefers value stocks, stocks that trade at a cheap price relative to their intrinsic value. A manager who followed a value bias has probably done particularly well over the past six or seven years, as value stocks have consistently beaten the market. But if gaining exposure to value constitutes a portfolio manager's entire investment approach, a hypothetical investor could have achieved similar performance at a much lower fee. All he or she would have needed to do was to purchase an exchange traded fund comprising value stocks. This is the essence of alpha/beta separation: disaggregating a manager's potential skill from the risks that he or she is taking. Understanding *how* a portfolio manager generates returns is as important as knowing what returns he or she generates.

Having laid out the various challenges facing the individual investor, in the second part of the book I focus on the uses and applications of the exchange traded fund. Much of this discussion is devoted to how exchange traded funds can be utilized to gain exposure to markets that provide significant diversification benefits. These include both international diversification and diversification into other asset classes, such as fixed-income instruments, commodities, and real estate. Continuing with the theme of diversification, I will move on to some of the more recent innovations in ETFs—products that offer the prospect of cheap and efficient financial exposure to everything from private equity to patent innovation. While these products are still relatively new, funds in this category are multiplying quickly and are likely to constitute a growing segment of the market for exchange traded funds. As I emphasize throughout the book, diversification is the one free lunch in finance—the one method that can improve your returns after accounting for risk.

The book concludes with a short look at some of the more sophisticated things you can do with exchange traded funds, such as leveraging your portfolio or profiting from negative insights (cases where you expect a particular market or sector to decline in value). Chapter 9 is meant primarily to round out the possibilities and flexibilities of the product, and should be treated with caution. The fact that a product *can* be used in a certain capacity does not mean it is appropriate or advisable for every user. This is particularly true of financial products, where failure to heed warning labels can be perilous.

This book is intended not only to enumerate the many challenges facing individual investors, but more important to provide some solutions, and in the process provide a new way for most people to think about their portfolios. While not a panacea, the ETF is an extremely flexible financial innovation that provides a much-needed alternative to traditional mutual funds. For many individuals, it will also present a much more reasonable alternative than attempting to build a portfolio by investing in individual stocks. One of the key messages of the early chapters is that if investors are finding it difficult to obtain above-average returns, either through their own stock picking or through actively managed mutual funds, they should focus more on their risk exposures and less on market-beating schemes. In other words, focus on the markets you want to own, rather than on how to beat them. Further value can be added through the relatively simple process of minimizing transaction costs. This is another area where institutional investors obsess, but which tends to be ignored by many retail investors. If you consider an average portfolio that you will contribute to over decades, even a small reduction in costs can add a considerable amount to its terminal value. As the returns on an investment are a function of both gains and costs, minimizing those costs is the simplest and easiest method of raising the overall return. An excellent way to lower costs is to focus on financial instruments that only charge for exposure to a market, rather than on the chimera of beating that market. In other words, look for funds, whether exchange traded or traditional index funds, that seek to replicate an index rather than beat it.

The approach outlined in this book seeks to find a middle ground between a completely passive approach of buying and holding a few index funds and a strategy based on security or fund selection. The aim is to construct more efficient portfolios, with efficiency defined as higher returns for a given level of overall risk, through the use of increased diversification and efficient implementation. A key component of this approach is finding markets and assets that are uncorrelated to the typical portfolio of large U.S.-based companies. The benefit of this approach is that often a disproportionate amount of a portfolio's volatility, or risk, is derived from an unnecessary concentration in similar securities. In the past, it was much more difficult to gain exposure to international markets or other asset classes such as commodities. ETFs make it considerably easier to gain exposure to these hitherto difficult-to-reach market segments. By adjusting strategic allocations toward a more diversified allocation, investors can add incremental returns with only a modest increase in risk. Unlike active stock picking, this is not a zero-sum game. Instead, incremental returns are obtained through the diversification benefits of combining assets that are relatively uncorrelated with each other.[4]

While some of the concepts discussed in the book will appear a bit abstract, they are actually critical to the discussion. Ideas such as alpha/beta separation, while mathematically intricate, derive from a simple concept investors would do well to internalize. Thinking about risk, and the sources of risk, will put the performance of your portfolio in a different light. Returns are no longer solely a function of a stock doing well or a fund performing poorly, but can also be expressed in terms of what risks that stock or fund represents. This framework will help in providing a context for evaluating the merits of different financial instruments, and for assessing how these services and instruments should be priced.

As chapter 2 illustrates, financial professionals are becoming ever more sophisticated in the design and implementation of their portfolios. Whether this has helped them obtain superior returns is still an issue open to academic debate, but at the very least, many of the new techniques have enabled professional investors to more adroitly manage risk. This is a useful point to remember. While the prospect of higher returns is generally what excites most investors, effective risk management is equally important in sustaining an investment plan for the long term.

While many of the techniques professional investors employ are beyond the resources of the average investor, individuals can enjoy many of the same advantages by developing a rudimentary understanding of risk management and transaction costs. It is in addressing these twin challenges—better risk control and more efficient implementation—that ETFs can offer the biggest advantage. A new financial instrument does not make an investor any smarter or more proficient in finding superior returns. That ability, as always, rests with the skills and insights of the individual. Indeed, no financial instrument will imbue an investor with insights he or she did not already possess. However, where exchange traded funds can add value is in allowing individuals to implement ideas and gain access to a plethora of different investment themes. As an added benefit, not only do they provide exposure to new market segments, but they do it in a cost-efficient manner. While that last sentence may not sound as exciting as many of the claims made in other investment books, as the last bear market demonstrated, excitement in your portfolio can be a mixed blessing.

PART 1

CHALLENGES

Chapter 1

REALISTIC RETURNS

B ack in the late 1990s, several surveys of investor sentiment suggested that while investors recognized the possibility of a bubble in stocks, they still held wildly optimistic expectations for their future performance. At the time, it was not unusual for investors to expect 20 percent annual returns in perpetuity. For those investors who were first introduced to stocks in the late 1990s, particularly those invested in large-cap U.S. stocks, this might have seemed a reasonable assumption based on their experience. The reality turned out to be quite different. For investors who entered the stock market in early 2000, much of this decade has proved a bit more difficult. While equity markets have rallied steadily since the bottom in 2002, U.S. large-cap stocks took seven years to eclipse their 2000 peak, leaving investors with only a paltry dividend yield of about 2 percent to sustain them. While some markets have fared better, equity returns have generally been lower this decade than during the previous two. What went wrong? The truth is nothing went wrong, except that many investors had forgotten that bear markets can and do occur, and that no fundamental law of physics guarantees 20 percent annual returns. In fact, some simple laws of economics more or less guarantee that the heady predictions for 20 percent returns were bound to disappoint.

This chapter will focus on what is realistic in financial markets. The argument for starting the book with such a broad theme is that expectations are critical when deciding how to manage your portfolio. Professional investors generally start with a very precise expectation of what their portfolio should return. They even go so far as to put the information on the marketing literature, along with the associated risks. Without specific return goals, any investor lacks context when assembling the different components of a portfolio. In order to generate that context, it is necessary to have some realistic expectation of market returns, which can then form a starting point for your own individual portfolio.

As most individual portfolios comprise mainly equities, this chapter focuses on what to expect from equity markets over the long term. If you know at the outset that world equity markets have generally provided a total return of around 7 percent to 10 percent, those expectations form an anchor in assessing your own financial goals. You may do a bit better than that average through careful management and a more aggressive stance, or a bit worse if you're defensive, but at least you have some feel for what's possible. Unfortunately, for most investors who have come of age over the past twenty years, a realistic sense of the long-term possibilities of equities is lacking. That is because the period from 1982 to 2000 was anything but typical. This chapter examines that period in an attempt to establish a more reasonable starting point for establishing realistic financial expectations.

The one defining characteristic of market bubbles is that they are obvious after the fact, but hard to identify while they're going on. Like most bubbles, the early impetus for the bull market began with significant improvements in the real economy. Beginning in the early 1980s, inflation and interest rates started to fall. By the 1990s, U.S. productivity had accelerated to its highest level in decades, and corporations were making unprecedented profits. However, by the late 1990s many world equity markets had become the embodiment of a classic speculative bubble, in which stock prices became completely unhinged from their underlying fundamentals. Wall Street legend has it that Joseph Kennedy knew it was time to get out of the stock market when the shoe shine boy began to give him stock advice. My own version of that story occurred in late 1999. One night I walked across the street to buy a Twinkie from the local small grocer. Unfortunately, the Twinkies were unavailable because the deliveryman who was supposed to be restocking the Hostess display was too busy trading options with his broker on his cell phone. I remember thinking that this was not a good sign. Sky-high price-to-earnings ratios, speculative message boards, and 300 percent gains on recent IPOs were one thing. Not being able to buy a Twinkie in the heart of New York because the deliveryman was trying to shave a sixteenth of a point on his Pets.com trade was, for me, the definition of a speculative bubble.

Investors today need to face the challenges of investing without the more-or-less consistent tailwind they enjoyed in the period between 1982 and 2000 (I say more or less as there were two bear markets in that period, in 1987 and 1990, both unusually brief). The 1980s and 1990s were a distinctly prosperous time for most investors. If you were invested in equity or bond markets during those decades, you could not help making money. From 1982 through 2000, financial markets enjoyed a once-in-a-generation period of stellar returns. The euphoria, of course, reached a crescendo in the final five years of the century, when market gains reached a magnitude and consistency rivaled only by the period leading up to the 1929 stock market crash.

It's critical for today's investors to understand how large those gains were in relation to normal market conditions. Of equal importance is quantifying why the conditions that led to those gains are unlikely to repeat themselves anytime in the near future. Start with a simple quantification of market gains based on the most popular index of large-cap U.S. equities, the S&P 500. Looking back over the last eighty years, monthly gains on the S&P 500 have averaged roughly 0.80 percent per month, excluding dividends (we will return to the dividend issue a bit later). Obviously, there has been a good amount of volatility around that average, but over the long term it has been consistent for the better part of eight decades. While stock markets can diverge from the fundamentals for long periods of time, ultimately the value of any security, and therefore the market in aggregate, is anchored by real economic activity. As economic growth is limited by its inputs, which include labor, capital, and productivity, there are natural limits on how fast economies can grow, which should exert some limits, at least over the long term, on financial assets.

NORMAL IN THE 1990s

Despite this long-term speed limit, markets can and do grow faster than economies, often for considerable periods. This is exactly what had happened by the later part of the last decade. By the time the millennial celebrations were in full swing, the S&P 500 had averaged gains of 2 percent a month for sixty consecutive months, or five

Source: Bloomberg

years. In other words, large-cap U.S. equities were appreciating at two and a half times their long-term average, and had been keeping up that pace for half a decade. The only other time in recent memory when this had occurred was in the summer of 1987. Prior to 1987, you need to go all the way back to the late 1920s to find a period when stocks gained that much for that long. So during the nearly two decades between the early 1980s and 2000, investors in U.S. stocks enjoyed not one but two separate five-year stretches when simply buying and holding an index of large-cap U.S. stocks produced gains in excess of 25 percent per year—an environment that had not existed for two generations of investors prior to those periods.

Now some could argue fairly that the gains on the S&P 500 were not representative of the overall market, as the late 1990s were dominated by a fetish for large-cap stocks, and that other segments of the market did not enjoy similar gains. There is some truth to this. Using the same methodology on the Russell 2000, an index of two thousand smaller U.S. companies, suggests smaller gains over the same period. While the advance in the Russell 2000 was significantly

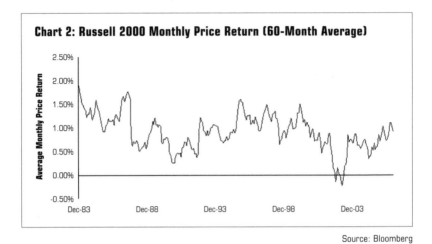

Chart 2: Russell 2000 Monthly Price Return (60-Month Average)

Source: Bloomberg

above average, it was not nearly as pronounced as in the large-cap universe. Indeed, one of the anomalies of the end of the 1990s bull market was how concentrated the gains were. By 1999, a disproportionate amount of the 25 percent annual gains were concentrated in a handful of large-cap equities, particularly technology stocks.

The counterpoint to the underperformance of small-cap stocks is the extent to which some market segments appreciated at an even more dizzying pace. While U.S. large-caps were gaining at roughly 2 percent a month, some sectors of that market were doing even better, in some cases much better. The price of technology shares, in particular, rose in a manner defying any economic or fundamental logic. The bubble in NASDAQ stocks has been well documented, yet given the sheer magnitude of the run-up in technology shares it is worth reiterating. The five-year average monthly gain for the NASDAQ Composite had reached an unprecedented 3 percent by the conclusion of 1999. By the late 1990s the relationship between technology stocks and their underlying fundamentals had become completely unhinged.

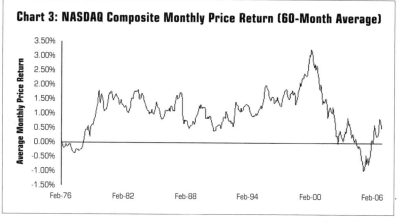

Source: Bloomberg

To put things in perspective, a 3 percent average monthly gain translates into a compound return of roughly 100 percent every two years. If this were a particular stock, and its price-to-earnings multiple (P/E) were to remain constant, this would indicate that the company's earnings would need to grow 100 percent in just two years. Now while there have been individual companies that have accomplished this feat, it is a rarity. However, the 3 percent returns described above are not for a particular stock, but for an entire market, comprising thousands of stocks. So in effect, investors who were bidding up NASDAQ stocks in the late 1990s either were making some outsized assumptions about earnings growth or were convinced that the "greater fool" theory would ensure that there was always another marginal buyer who would take the shares off their hands. Returns of that rate are rare, and often unjustified in individual stocks, but are the stuff of legend for an entire market index, particularly one in a developed country.

And while financial crises such as the Asian contagion of 1997 and the Russian default of 1998 resulted in significant dislocations in many foreign markets, international equities still managed to put on an impressive show during the concluding years of the 1990s. The MSCI World Index appreciated by nearly 1.5 percent a month, on average, during the period from 1995 to 2000. So while magnitudes did differ, and international securities and U.S. small-cap names trailed U.S. large-cap and technology shares, virtually all equity markets luxuriated in a prolonged period of coordinated growth. This period was defined by gains that were significantly above their long-term averages and persisted for many years. In short, the period that witnessed the rise of the U.S. retail investor was in no way indicative of normal market conditions. Instead, it was a once-in-a-generation confluence of good fundamentals and giddy speculation.

THE DEBT THAT EQUITY INVESTORS OWED
TO THE BOND MARKET

Some pundits have argued that there is no physical law to prevent the good times from continuing. As of this writing, the world economy is robust, interest rates and inflation remain low, and financial liquidity is more than ample. With some justification, they can point to a four-plus-year bull market, already one of the longest on record. Indeed, the optimists list a host of reasons to support another prolonged bull market and the potential for similar gains in the near term, including: the fall of communism and a more inclusive world labor market, the accelerating pace of technological innovation, a more stable business cycle, and in some ways, a more stable geopolitical environment.

While all of these factors should theoretically reduce risk and potentially raise earnings, they are still unlikely to lead to the same type of appreciation witnessed in the 1980s and 1990s. There are two reasons for this. First, stocks were considerably cheaper at the start of the 1982 bull market than they have been at any time since. In other words, when the bull market began twenty-five years ago, stocks were trading at bargain basement prices. Second, not only did earnings surge in the 1980s and 1990s, but so did valuations. Much of the rise in valuations, or earnings multiples, can be attributed to a onetime secular, or long-term, decline in inflation. Having already occurred, a similar drop in inflation cannot provide a second tailwind for stocks. In fact, with inflation already in the 2 percent to 3 percent range, any meaningful drop in inflation from current levels would be indicative of deflation, not necessarily a plus for equity investors.

The first argument against another 1982–2000 bull market is the price of shares today versus their level in 1982. Twenty-five years ago, at the start of the last bull market, you could buy the S&P 500 index for just eight times earnings. In other words, investors were only willing to pay eight times the previous year's earnings for large-cap U.S. stocks. In contrast, at the peak of the bubble, that measure of value had expanded to more than thirty, a quadrupling of valuations. So in 2000, investors were willing to pay four times more for a given stream of earnings than they were eighteen years prior.

What changed in investors' minds to produce that large a revision of what constituted fair value for stocks? In general, the U.S. economy staged a significant turnaround over the intervening eighteen years. On a host of metrics, ranging from inflation to productivity, things did indeed get much better, not just in the United States but throughout much of the world. Central bankers succeeded in reining in the inflation of the 1970s, entire industries were deregulated, the Cold War ended with a subsequent drop in military spending, and productivity, which affects corporate earnings, surged for the first time in decades. So like most bubbles, the 1982–2000 bull market began and was sustained by a real and significant improvement in the economic and financial fundamentals. The market should have been more expensive after the changes described above. The problem was that speculative excess took things too far. Even after accounting for lower inflation, better productivity growth, and a more stable geopolitical environment, it is hard to argue that investors should have been paying four times more for the same earnings stream than they were twenty years prior.

Since 2000, market valuations have been generally heading lower. U.S. stocks are currently trading at just half the valuations they were at seven years ago. Even though valuations continued to accelerate into 2002, because of a collapse in corporate earnings, they have subsequently been contracting since 2003. While markets have posted respectable gains, corporate America has been growing even faster. U.S. companies have generated a record string of consecutive double-digit earnings gains. The recent strength in corporate earnings has also pushed down valuations, as earnings have grown faster than stock prices. However, while multiples have indeed normalized, they only appear exceptionally cheap when compared to the inflated levels of the mid-1980s and 1990s. The S&P 500 currently trades for 17.5 times trailing twelve-month reported earnings (i.e., the price of the index is 17.5 times the index's earnings per share over the previous twelve-month period), a level exactly in line with the long-term fifty-year average. And while it is fair to argue that stocks should have a higher multiple given the relatively low level of inflation and interest rates, no level of adjust-

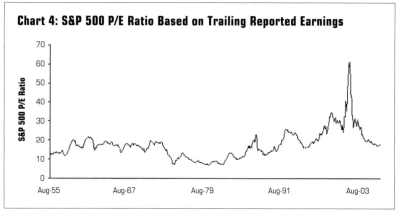

Chart 4: S&P 500 P/E Ratio Based on Trailing Reported Earnings

Source: Bloomberg

ment would suggest that stocks are unusually cheap, as they arguably were back in 1982.

The second obstacle to a 1990s-style bull market is that equity markets have become victims of their own success. One of the primary drivers of the expansion in multiples during the 1980s and 1990s was the steady drop in long-term interest rates. This drop in rates was in turn due to the effectiveness of the world's central banks in stemming the inflation of the 1970s. One of the main reasons stocks were so cheap in 1982 was that people had lost faith in the government's ability to control inflation and maintain the value of the currency. When the S&P 500 was trading at barely eight times earnings in the summer of 1982, the yield on the 10-year U.S. Treasury note was 14 percent. In contrast, by the time the multiple on the S&P 500 had climbed to thirty-two times earnings in the summer of 2000, long-term rates in the United States were less than half of those levels.

For the better part of twenty years, the secular decline in long-term interest rates went hand in hand with a gradual but steady increase in the market's price-to-earnings multiple. This relationship is exactly what you would expect from textbook theory. Stock prices are valued based on expected earnings and a discount rate that converts those future earnings to their current value. As the discount rate used for stocks is largely a function of overall market rates, lower interest rates have the effect of raising stock prices. A long-term drop in bond yields should logically drive stock prices, and valuations, higher. This is because future corporate earnings are worth more today when the discount rate, that is, the interest rate, is lower. (This relationship makes sense when you think about the math. To calculate a present value of a future earnings stream, you divide the future earnings by a discount rate. The lower the rate, which is the denominator in the equation, the more those future earnings are worth today.)

Another illustration of this relationship is contained in the next chart. It compares market multiples and interest rates going back to the 1950s. Each point on the chart marks a monthly observation of the S&P 500 market multiple and the yield on the 10-year Treasury. As can be seen, as rates fall, the stock market's valuation generally increases. The accompanying equation on the chart indicates that the level of interest rates can explain approximately 20 percent of the variation in market multiples over the past fifty years. The form of the equation also suggests that the relationship is nonlinear, indicating that the impact of falling interest rates is somewhat dependent on the levels of interest rates. Historically, the biggest increases in multiples have occurred when rates were particularly low, with the impact less significant when rates were very high. In other words, if interest rates fall from 11 percent to 10 percent, the drop should have a smaller impact on the market's earnings multiple

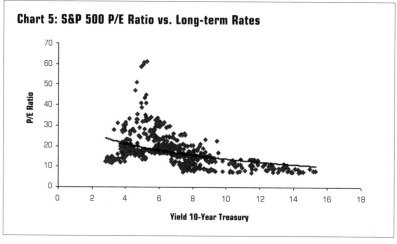

Chart 5: S&P 500 P/E Ratio vs. Long-term Rates

than a drop from 6 percent to 5 percent. Regardless of the nuances of the relationship, it is clear that falling interest rates were one of the principal drivers of the rise in market valuations witnessed during the bull market.

Another way to examine the relationship between interest rates and multiples is to take a step back and examine the principal determinant of long-term rates, inflation. The previous section outlined the relationship between long-term U.S. interest rates and equity valuations. What happens to the relationship when we decompose interest rates further? In the above example, I used the yield on the 10-year U.S. Treasury note. As these instruments are issued by the U.S. government, they contain no credit risk (i.e., investors in these bonds can be confident that the government will pay the interest and principal on the bond). Instead, the prevailing interest rate is determined by two factors: a "real interest rate" and an expectation for future inflation. The real interest rate is what a lender would charge for interest in the absence of any inflation, or expectations of inflation, and is generally assumed to be between 2 percent and 3 percent. So if a Treasury note was trading at a yield of 6 percent, and assuming a 3 percent real yield, 3 percent (6 percent minus the 3 percent real interest rate) would represent an investor's best guess of what inflation will be during the life of that instrument. The inflation expectation component of a bond is heavily influenced by recent inflationary trends. In other words, if inflation levels have recently been high, bond yields are also likely to be high as investors extrapolate recent trends into the future (think of the mid-1980s: even after inflation started to fall, bond yields stayed high as investors remained skeptical of a prolonged period of low inflation).

For this reason, current inflation levels have a significant influence on bond yields, and in turn, on how stocks are valued. Generally, higher inflation translates into lower valuations, just as higher bond yields had a similar effect. Going back over the past fifty years, periods of high inflation have generally been associated with lower earnings multiples for the market. Conversely, when inflation has been low, as it was for most of the 1990s, equity investors have generally been willing to pay a premium for stocks in the form of higher price-to-earnings ratios.

Again, using a scatter plot to quantify the relationship, changes in core inflation have a significant impact on the level of the S&P 500's P/E ratio. Similar to the case with interest rates, the relationship is best described by a nonlinear model. As with interest rates, when inflation is low, the relationship has a more dramatic impact on market multiples than when inflation is high. For example, according to this model, if inflation dropped from 12 percent to 10 percent, the P/E ratio for the S&P 500 should go from roughly ten times last year's earnings to approximately eleven times earn-

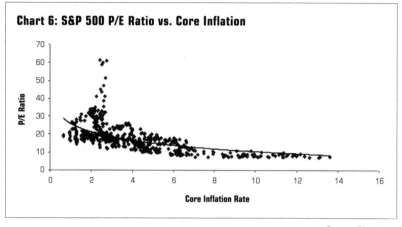

Chart 6: S&P 500 P/E Ratio vs. Core Inflation

Source: Bloomberg

ings. However, if inflation is already at a low level, a similar 2 percent drop would have a much more dramatic impact. If inflation fell from 5 percent to 3 percent, the model suggests market multiples should rise from fifteen times earnings to more than eighteen times earnings. In other words, when inflation is high, a 2 percent drop in inflation causes market valuations to rise by 10 percent, but when inflation is already low a similar drop should result in a 20 percent rise in the market's value. This is exactly what happened in the 1990s. The nineties witnessed a continuation of the secular decline in inflation that began in the early 1980s under Paul Volcker's stewardship of the U.S. Federal Reserve. As core inflation declined from approximately 6 percent in the late 1980s toward 2 percent a decade later, investors were willing to pay a consistently higher multiple for equities.

So if inflation and interest rates are still low, what is the problem? Doesn't the market look reasonable given the favorable economic conditions? The problem is that even low levels of inflation and interest rates never fully justified the market's peak at the end of the last bull market. By the closing year of the twentieth century, the P/E ratio of the S&P 500 had climbed into the low thirties, an unprecedented number. Even when taking into account the low level of inflation and interest rates, this appeared excessive. Using the above models, based on both interest rates and inflation, would have suggested that "fair value" for the S&P 500 would have been a multiple closer to twenty than thirty. This can be seen by examining the previous charts. The curved lines through the data provide an indication of the theoretical "fair value" that the market should trade on based on the long-term relationship between inflation and interest rates. While there is no physical or economic law that demands that markets trade at these levels, it can be viewed as a rough gauge of how the level of rates or inflation should impact valuations. When you look at those relationships, even very low levels of inflation and interest rates suggest a market valuation in the low twenties. This stands in sharp contrast to the market's eventual peak in valuations, which reached more than thirty times trailing earnings, roughly 50 percent above fair value. So for all the prognosticators who argued that stocks were fairly valued given the benign macroenvironment, it appears that even a decade-low rate of inflation did not justify what investors were willing to pay for large-cap stocks at the end of the 1990s.

THE ROLE OF PRODUCTIVITY AND DIVIDENDS

If inflation and interest rates cannot sufficiently explain the run-up in valuations during the end of the last decade, was there another fundamental justification for the record-high valuations? One of the other oft-cited explanations was the pickup in productivity. U.S. productivity, which measures economic output per hour worked, soared

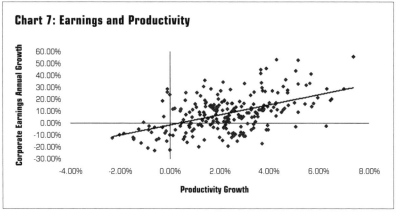

Source: Bloomberg

during the latter half of the 1990s. Many explanations have been posited, including a delayed reaction to the technology buildup, globalization, more efficient inventory and supply management, and better corporate management. Whatever the exact causes, rising productivity is an unambiguous positive for the economy and the stock market. As companies can produce higher output with the same number of workers, corporate profits tend to rise. Chart 8 illustrates the relationship. As productivity rises, the rate at which corporate profits grow also tends to increase. Productivity growth can account for more than 25 percent of the variation in U.S. corporate earnings.

As discussed previously, the theoretical speed limit for earnings growth is tied to the overall rate of GDP growth, which is itself dependent upon population growth and productivity. As long-term productivity rises, expectations for future earnings growth should also rise. Faster growth translates into higher future earnings, which should indicate a higher price for stocks. As long as productivity is accelerating, investors are justified in their expectation of better corporate profits, so it is reasonable that they are willing to accept higher earnings multiples for a claim on those profits. As earnings gains quicken, investors

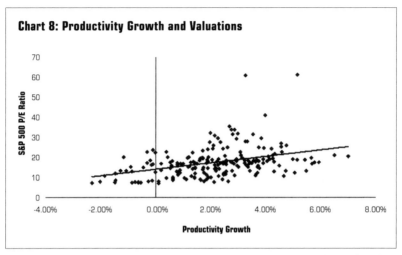

Source: Bloomberg

should be more willing to pay a higher premium or multiple as the market's earnings will compound more quickly.

Again, the empirical data conforms to the theory. The positive impact of productivity on corporate earnings does indeed translate into investors' willingness to pay a higher price for stocks (i.e., higher P/E ratios). Periods of higher productivity growth have historically been associated with periods of higher earnings multiples, although, here again, the numbers come up short when trying to justify the record valuations of the previous decade. While the productivity surge of the late 1990s justified higher P/E ratios, it only works to a point. Even after accounting for higher productivity, we are still hard pressed to account for the market multiple climbing above the low twenties.

So while the fundamentals of the 1990s were, to quote Voltaire's Dr. Pangloss, the "best of all possible worlds," it would still appear that equities, at least in the United States, were significantly overvalued by the end of the decade. Even after accounting for a benign economic environment characterized by low inflation, low interest rates, and high productivity, the valuations of U.S. large-cap stocks had become unmoored from all traditional economic relationships.

Before concluding, one final point needs to be addressed. So far we have examined market returns purely from the perspective of capital gains. However, historically, a significant amount of the total return from investing in equities came from dividends. During the twentieth century, reinvested dividends accounted for approximately 41 percent of total stock market return—the exception being the second half of the 1990s. During that period, dividends accounted for less than 10 percent of the total return for stocks.[1] In January 2000, the dividends on the S&P 500 equaled just 1.2 percent of the price of the index, far below the 4.7 percent that is the historical average. Given the historically pivotal role of dividends in supporting equity market returns, it is curious that investors continue to expect returns above the long-term average when one of the principal sources of those returns is so far below the long-term average. Dividends have normally represented the dominant part of the average return on stocks. The reliable return attributable to dividends, not the less predictable portion arising from capital gains, is the main reason stocks have historically been a good long-term investment.[2] With the dividend yield dropping to and remaining near historic lows, investors face an additional obstacle to higher returns. Not only are valuations considerably above the levels that prevailed at the start of the last bull market, but with dividend yields less than half of their historical levels, another source of potential return has been removed.

A cursory look at the table on page 38 illustrates this. The table looks at the role of dividends in U.S. stock returns. As illustrated, in

PERIOD	PRICE RETURNS	DIVIDEND RETURNS	TOTAL RETURN	DIVIDEND CONTRIBUTION TO TOTAL RETURN
1926–1929	13.86%	5.78%	19.64%	29.43%
1930s	-5.26%	6.23%	0.97%	NA
1940s	2.98%	5.75%	8.73%	65.86%
1950s	13.58%	5.63%	19.21%	29.31%
1960s	4.39%	3.36%	7.75%	43.35%
1970s	1.60%	4.28%	5.88%	72.79%
1980s	12.59%	4.96%	17.55%	28.26%
1990s	15.31%	2.90%	18.21%	15.93%
2000–2005	-2.68%	1.59%	-1.09%	NA

Source: Standard & Poor's as of 12/31/05 (taken from Legg Mason, "A Case for Dividend Investing: Understanding the Historical Perspective—and Evolving Trends in Equity Markets," 6/06).

most decades dividends accounted for somewhere between 30 percent and 70 percent of the return on U.S. equities. In other words, if stocks returned roughly 10 percent per year, 3 percent to 7 percent of that return came from the dividend yield rather than any capital appreciation on the shares. That reliable pattern began to change in the 1990s, when dividends accounted for less than 20 percent of the return on stocks. The current dividend yield on U.S. stocks is now even lower than it was in the 1990s. With dividend yields stuck well below their long-term average, investors should be even more cautious in their expectations of what the stock market can deliver.

GOING FORWARD, WHAT TO EXPECT

As all of the above has been documented ad nauseam over the past six years, why bring it up in the context of challenges facing individual investors? Obviously, those who lost money during the bubble have already suffered their losses, and investors who bought at the market bottom in 2002 have been well rewarded. The reason for reiterating this bit of financial history is to illustrate why nineties-style gains should not figure into anyone's expectation of future market returns. The gains of the 1990s, and to a lesser extent the 1980s, were predicated on trends that are unlikely to, and in one case cannot, repeat themselves.

The quadrupling of market multiples between 1982 and 2000 was heavily predicated on the eighteen-year bull market in bonds and the coincident collapse in inflation. With long-term yields in the United States in the mid-4-percent range, a similar decline in long-term interest rates is mathematically impossible. The best we can hope for is a period of sustained low rates. Real interest rates (interest rates minus the rate of inflation) are at around 2 percent to 2.5 percent. Historically, they have been a bit above this level, with long-term rates in the United States averaging about 2.7 percent above the level of core inflation. With interest rates already at a relatively tight spread to inflationary pressures, a significant drop in yields is unlikely absent a recession. A recession would also bring about an end to the recent period of stellar earnings growth; so a sharp economic contradiction, even if it did provide for a drop in long-term rates, is an unwelcome contingency for the stock market.

There is also the realistic possibility that inflation could accelerate. Commodity prices, particularly energy, have been rising sharply for five years. Some of the rise is a result of scarcity of supply and long-term emerging market demand, neither of which may reverse in the short term. In addition, the dollar has been on a mostly downward trajectory for the better part of five years. Both of these trends, a lower dollar and higher commodity prices, are inherently inflationary. When coupled with the lagged effect of a prolonged period of cheap money, modestly higher inflation is not hard to imagine. Even a relatively small rise in the core inflation rate to 3 percent would be a bit of a shock to financial markets, which have become accustomed to flat inflation and stable long-term rates.

It would seem that neither a drop in inflation nor a drop in interest rates is likely to bail out the stock market, so what about productivity? Unfortunately, recently productivity has been heading the wrong way. And while there is the possibility of productivity remaining elevated for a prolonged period, absent another surge, the market's current valuation already discounts robust productivity. So the two key tailwinds of the 1982 to 2000 bull market have been removed.

None of this is to suggest that equity markets will not have future, often prolonged, periods of superior performance. Although not cheap by the standards of 1982, market multiples are reasonable when compared to the long-term averages. However, there are a few reality checks that investors should keep in mind when evaluating future equity returns. First, investors who were fortunate, or old, enough to invest at the start of the bull market in the 1980s were able to get in at a period when market multiples were unusually low, roughly half of today's levels. Second, much of the subsequent multiple expansion was driven by a once-in-a-generation reduction in interest rates, a reduction that by its very definition cannot occur a second time. Third, and related to the second point, this drop in rates was primarily driven by a drop in long-term inflation expectations justified by the slow but steady drop in core inflation. With core inflation now down around 2.5 percent, a further drop is neither realistic nor desirable. Fourth, multiple expansion was further aided by an upward shift in productivity. Forecasts for future productivity growth are well beyond the scope of this book. Suffice it to say that even if productivity were to remain in the 2 percent to 3 percent range, which would be a significant increase over its long-run average, the historical relationship between productivity and market multiples would suggest that the market is already fairly priced.

Given the current market opportunities, which are not bad but also not as good as they have been, investors should be cautious in their expectations. To a large extent, the market is a victim of its own success. Economic conditions today represent a huge improvement from where they were twenty-five years ago, but therein lies the problem. The irony of financial markets is that the best buying opportunities occur when things are at their worst. Today's investors have the misfortune of starting at a time when the world economy is exceptionally robust and stable. So before extrapolating the gains of the last few years, or the last few decades, it is worth remembering the series of conditions that produced those gains. While markets will have both good and bad years, and long-term investing in equities is still one of the best investments, investors need to have a realistic sense of the possible, which generally does not include 25 percent annual gains.

Chapter 2

INCREASING SOPHISTICATION

If individual investors can no longer count on the tailwind of ever rising multiples to lift their portfolios, what are the prospects for adding incremental returns through stock or manager selection? Even if market returns are lower than they were in the eighties and nineties, can individual investors improve their overall returns by selecting stocks that perform better than the market or hiring investment managers to pick stocks for them? In this chapter, we'll examine the case for individuals' outperforming the benchmark averages, both from a historical perspective and also by trying to take a look at their principal competition, institutional investors.

RETAIL INVESTORS VERSUS THE MARKET: THE EMPIRICAL EVIDENCE

So how have individual investors traditionally fared in their ability to beat the market by picking stocks? In order to be clear in what we are discussing, I will define beating the market, or *outperformance,* as the ability to generate excess returns over some benchmark or index. As will be highlighted in chapter 3, this is actually an artificially easy standard, as it ignores risk. An investor may outperform a benchmark by simply holding a portfolio of assets that are more risky than the overall market. This approach will generally lead to superior returns in rising markets, such as we had for most of the eighties and nineties. Holding riskier assets does not imply any greater skill, but simply a greater propensity to take on risk. But for the time being, we will ignore the more sophisticated definition, and focus on the simpler question of whether individuals can significantly outperform the broader market through stock picking.

Investors face a formidable challenge when looking for a security to buy. There are more than ten thousand securities to choose from, and this is just for investors focused on U.S. assets. The number expands significantly when the opportunity set is opened up to international stocks. Even when focused on a smaller universe of stocks, such as the S&P 500, there is still a larger array of options than most retail investors are equipped to deal with. Given the vast number of choices, it is not surprising that investors tend to focus on securities to which their attention has been drawn, such as stocks that are frequently highlighted on television or in the financial press.[1] While different bits of information attract different investors, most of us are unlikely to have a systematic process for evaluating a company's prospects or its relative value. Very few individual investors have formulated a precise approach to investing. More often, investors are likely to be drawn to individual securities based on news stories or similarly random recommendations.

There is another bias in investor behavior that often hampers their performance. Securities that have performed well in the recent past, so-called momentum stocks, are more likely to be the focus of media and popular attention, and thus become the focus of individual investors. Without a disciplined approach to temper their emotions, investors, both retail and institutional, tend toward overconfidence. It is this overconfidence, as much as lack of formal training and inferior information, that leads to poor performance.[2] Professional investors are not immune to this bias, but they benefit from the discipline of a clearly articulated investment process. An investor who has specific rules and criteria for stock selection will at least be able to mitigate some of the damage done by human emotion and overconfidence.

Finally, there is one additional disadvantage that impedes the returns of individual investors. Retail investors tend to limit their options when investing to only purchasing securities, a tendency known as *long-only investing*. Like traditional mutual funds, most individual investors do not short securities. Shorting a security involves betting against a stock's performance by selling borrowed shares in an attempt to benefit from a decline in price. The technique allows investors to profit from insights into poorly performing companies. Suppose you had a very negative view of a stock. If you could only purchase securities, or "go long," the most negative statement you could make on the stock would be to avoid adding it to your portfolio. In effect, you would be underweighting this stock in your portfolio, as it would have some positive weight, let's say 2 percent, in its benchmark index, but no weight in your individual portfolio. The problem is that most securities have only a minuscule weight in a given index, often less than 0.10 percent of the index value. So when trying to outperform an index such as the S&P 500, a long-only investor is very limited in his or her ability to express a negative view. If all you can do with a stock you hate is not own it, and that stock has only a tiny weight in the index you're trying to beat, right or wrong your decision will have only a negligible impact on your performance relative to that benchmark.

However, if you shorted the security, and it subsequently declined, you would profit by the amount of the decline. If you sold 1,000 shares short and the stock declined from $50 to $45, you would have made a profit of $5,000, minus the cost of borrowing the stock. Compare this scenario with the one above, where the only way you could express a negative opinion was by simply not purchasing the stock. In that instance, you avoided a loss but failed to make a profit. Without the ability to short, an investor's opportunity to gain from negative information is very limited. When compared to more nimble investors, such as the ever growing hedge fund community, retail investors are disadvantaged in their unwillingness to embrace short selling. In a study on retail investment habits, less than 1 percent of sales in the data set were short sales.[3] This limitation is not trivial. Recent research on the gains in portfolio efficiency from shorting suggest that the removal of the long-only constraint leads to significant improvements, both in cumulative returns and in risk-adjusted returns.[4] Until more retail investors learn this lesson, they are at a significant disadvantage to more sophisticated, and flexible, professional investors, particularly hedge funds.

The net result of these cognitive biases and behavioral headwinds is a consistent track record of failing to outperform the market. Most academic studies of retail investors reinforce this picture, whether they focus on longer-term investing or shorter-term trading. Even in the case of those retail investors whom you would imagine to be more sophisticated, the results are largely the same. In a study of day traders, whose popularity rose and plummeted in the late 1990s, the results were no different. At first glance, it would be reasonable to expect this class of individuals to perform better, as unlike their more casual counterparts, they are quasi-professionals who are devoting some or all of their time to trading the markets. Yet even for these individuals the results were discouraging. One study of day traders in Taiwan demonstrated that while most did earn a profit, those profits were insufficient to cover their trading costs. Even worse, in a typical six-month period, more than eight out of ten day traders lost money.[5]

The poor performance of Taiwanese day traders is not a local phenomenon or one limited to those weaving in and out of the market every few seconds. The same challenges and cognitive mistakes hurt longer-term investors as well. Even during the late 1990s, when investors enjoyed one of the most benign investing environments in that century, the results were largely the same. In particular, investors cheated themselves out of many of those stellar gains by churning, or trading their portfolios too often. Most investors trade too much, and sell too early. A study of individual trading data accumulated from discount brokerages in the 1990s suggested that the average stock-trading household turned over 75 percent of its portfolio every year. Generally, these people were selling out of the more profitable stocks, and replacing them with worse-performing names. This habit of selling winners had a significantly negative impact on performance.[6]

Once again, psychology and the lack of any systematic approach wound up hurting investors. Most studies confirm that investors tend to make very similar mistakes, mistakes that are exacerbated in the absence of any self-disciplining investment plan. The average investor in the above study underperformed the market as a result. Investors showed a lack of ability in both market timing and stock selection. Generally, they overestimated their abilities to pick stocks by selling at the wrong time and replacing their stocks with generally poorer performers.[7]

None of the above suggests that individuals can never beat the market. The survey of the Taiwanese day traders did indicate that a small group, the top 10 percent, managed to consistently earn positive excess returns. But for those taking solace in that fact, remember that barely one out of ten individuals was able to consistently profit from the market, even when this was their sole focus. That is a discouraging statistic for the overwhelming number of investors who have jobs outside of watching the market's next tick. If nothing else, the above example should help illustrate the magnitude of the task set out for anyone who is trying to add excess returns through stock selection. Even for those individuals solely focused on the task, only a small minority tend to succeed at it. While everyone would like to believe they are in that upper 10 percent, that is probably not a sound assumption on which to build an investment philosophy. Individuals who insist on picking stocks without the requisite skills and resources are only eroding their investment returns. As Carrie Fisher famously said in *When Harry Met Sally*, "Everyone thinks they have good taste and a sense of humor, but they can't possibly all have good taste." The same can be said about picking stocks.

INSTITUTIONAL INVESTORS: WHY METEOROLOGISTS, ONCOLOGISTS, AND GEOLOGISTS SUDDENLY HAVE JOBS AT HEDGE FUNDS

If the above evidence has not convinced you to reconsider the merits of trying to pick stocks, it is probably worth taking a closer look at the competition. The previous discussion alluded to structural reasons why retail investors struggle to outperform the market. These reasons include behavioral biases, such as too much attention to momentum stocks, as well as self-imposed limitations on their investment techniques. Yet even without these disadvantages, retail investors would still face an uphill struggle against the competition: institutional investors. Even the most ardent weekend warrior realizes deep down that he probably could not hit a major league fastball, or last a round with a professional heavyweight boxer. But most people do not see a similar contradiction in trying to beat the market through security selection—even though this is another example of the amateur attempting to compete with a better resourced and more focused professional. For the same reasons you are unlikely to last a round with the heavyweight fighter, there is a similar challenge in trying to beat a market increasingly dominated by sophisticated institutional investors in what is ostensibly a zero-sum game.

This was not always the case. The increasing dominance of institutional investors is a relatively recent phenomenon. In a recent study by the Conference Board, institutional investors—defined as pension funds, investment companies, insurance companies, banks, and foundations—controlled $24.1 trillion in assets as of 2005. This is up from a low of $17.3 trillion in 2002. Indeed, institutions have been steadily growing as a percentage of the overall market. By 2005, institutions held a record 61.2 percent of U.S. equities, up from 51.4 percent in 2000. For larger U.S. companies, the percentage is even higher. Institutional ownership of the largest one thousand companies rose from less than 62 percent in 2000 to nearly 68 percent by 2005.[8]

The increase in the relative size of institutional ownership means that increasingly an individual's competition for above-average returns is not with his or her neighbor but with the highly paid and well-funded mutual fund or hedge fund manager. Among the categories of institutional investors described above, the mutual fund manager has garnered the largest gains among institutional managers. Back in 1980, the still clubby mutual fund business accounted for less than 3 percent of institutional assets. A quarter century later, mutual funds' percentage of institutional assets grew by nearly ten-fold to 23.8 percent. This growth occurred mostly at the expense of bank and trust companies, which witnessed their share of the mix drop from 38.8 percent to below 12 percent by 2005.[9] The change in the composition of investors has a profound impact on the overall investment landscape. Institutions employ different types of strategies from individual investors, and also trade differently. As their relative percentage of the overall marketplace has grown, it has the net effect of creating a more competitive, or in industry terminology, "efficient" marketplace.

Given the prevalence and heft of the professional money management industry, it is worth examining who they are, how they approach financial markets, and what advantages they have over the retail investor. This sketch of the methods and resources of the professional investor illustrates the extent to which money managers will go in their efforts to beat the market. The competitive threat of the professional is of critical importance for the individual investor. Whenever an investor purchases a stock, he or she is implicitly betting that the security will outperform a broader index of similar stocks. If not, why buy the stock, rather than just an index fund representing a broader, more diversified basket of securities? As a market index is made up of numerous securities, some of which will do better and some worse than the average, individual stock selection implies an ability to differentiate between the winners and the losers. In order to be in the former camp, an investor must have more skill, or luck, than their competition. And while institutional investors have had their own mixed record in beating the market, for the most part they begin with vastly superior resources and a process that most individual investors would find difficult to replicate.

Let's turn first to the issue of process. As mentioned previously, one of the principal advantages of a professional money manager is a well-defined process that provides a framework for selecting securities, building a portfolio, and implementing trades. Quantitative money managers, or quants, represent a good example of this process-driven approach. Quantitative managers are one of the fastest-growing segments of the money management industry. Based on a recent management consulting study, by the end of 2004, there were seventy quantitatively managed accounts and commingled funds. Those seventy accounts, which had an established track record, managed $157 billion, nearly double the assets under management from a similar study three years earlier. This represented an annualized rate of growth of 21 percent in the three years to 2004, versus a growth rate of just 9 percent for the non-quant products.[10] This trend has accelerated in recent years. Several factors, from improved performance during the bear market to cheaper and more accessible computer power, help to explain the rise of the quant. Key among these advantages is the application of a systematic and objective approach to managing money.

Relying on mathematical models to drive the investment process, the quantitative discipline seeks to adapt the rigors of the scientific method to the often murky world of investments and economics. The adaptation of these methods provides a number of advantages over more traditional, qualitative techniques. First, the application of scientific methods to investing allows portfolio managers and analysts to test an investment thesis before actually committing capital. The quant does this by building computer models that test various financial theories, which are in turn based on different mathematical relationships. The mathematical and statistical techniques allow a fund manager to deconstruct the complexity of financial markets into a manageable list of factors and relationships, and then use those factors in a systematic fashion to build investment portfolios. Like all models of the real world, even the most complex models are a gross simplification of reality. The role of the math is not to perfectly represent the real world. Instead, it is to reduce the decisions involved, not to mathematical certainty, but to mathematical representation, and to capture as many of the critical bits of reality as possible. The reality that quants are attempting to capture is which factors are relevant for picking stocks, and how to combine these factors into one holistic process.

The other advantage of the quantitative process is that it is so well defined. This is not a trivial issue, as all investors, both individual and institutional, tend to have behavioral biases that impede their ability to follow a disciplined process. Emotions generally work to the detriment of investors, which is one reason institutions focus so heavily on developing a process that can help to minimize the emotional aspects of investing. While professional money managers are not infallible, having to articulate a definitive process helps minimize the emotional aspect and provides an advantage most individual investors lack. These emotional biases are one of the reasons that individual investors have tended to trail behind the market benchmarks. From 1984 through 2002, individuals earned just 2.6 percent versus the S&P 500's gain of 12.2 percent. Research in the United States has demonstrated that this dramatic underperformance is largely a function of behavioral mistakes.[11]

In addition to a better-defined process, institutional investors generally know a lot more about the stocks they are buying than you do. While quants have turned investing into a science, all institutional investors, quants and traditional stock pickers alike, tend to enjoy superior information. I'm not speaking about insider information, which per recent scandals is still apparently prevalent in financial markets, but information that is in the public domain, but is too diffused or obscure to be readily available to the average investor. Institutional investors have vast resources to find, gather, and process information concerning specific industries and stocks. Most professional money managers will go to extraordinary lengths to obtain just a small nugget of information that gives them an advantage over other managers. A few examples will help illustrate the information deficit that an average retail investor is facing when competing against a well-funded money manager.

Consider the case of investing in the energy sector. Natural gas prices are largely driven by weather-related factors during the winter months. Even a slightly better than average knowledge of the likelihood of short-term weather patterns would be an enormous advantage in trading stocks in the natural gas industry. Therefore, some large institutions will do whatever possible to gain any weather-related insights. One instance of a hedge fund attempting to ostensibly predict the weather is Citadel, one of the largest and most successful hedge funds in the industry. Some years back, it was announced that the firm had four meteorologists on staff, a seemingly strange hiring practice for a financial services firm. The hiring makes a great deal more sense in the context of the firm's energy trading business. Back in 2001, when Enron imploded and other energy traders were leaving the business, Citadel's founder, Ken Griffin, pushed into energy trading. Today, Citadel employs a seventy-member team, including four meteorologists, who trade natural gas and power.[12] Considering the firm's assets, estimated at over $10 billion, keeping four meteorologists on staff seems like a very modest investment in information. To the extent that those meteorologists can even slightly increase the firm's odds of assessing weather patterns, that information can be leveraged to create a huge advantage in trading energy-related assets.

This willingness to employ industry experts, both inside and outside the firm, is a growing trend. While not every hedge fund or mutual fund keeps an army of meteorologists on staff, they are increasingly willing to turn to outside consultants to fill that gap. Hedge funds are well known for purchasing data and consulting services from industry experts. For example, investors in the health care sector will pay large sums to doctors and other medical researchers to gain insights into the prospects for a new drug or medical treatment. In many cases, these funds will pay up to $1 million a year to firms known as matchmakers. These consulting firms pair up investment firms with doctors involved in drug research. Gerson Lehrman, the largest such consultant, claims to have sixty thousand doctors available to speak with their investment clients.[13] The doctors can provide expert advice as to the nuances of a potential new drug, as well as the key issues likely to determine its efficacy and ultimate approval by the FDA. The next time you buy a pharmaceutical stock based on the prospects for that company's new drug, it is worth considering how much information you have on the drug, versus the hedge fund manager who just spoke to a PhD in oncology who explained why the drug compound is never likely to work.

And even with all of this information, investment managers still tend to be more disciplined and specific in their investments than individual investors. They are cognizant of the fact that whenever they attempt to compete in a segment of the market where they do not have an edge in information or methodology, another more sophisticated institution is going to have the advantage. For most individual investors there is no predefined limit on where or in what they can invest. As ideas come to them they may take some and discard others, but it is unlikely that they start with a strict limit on their investment options. In contrast, the majority of professional investors place a number of self-imposed constraints on the types of securities they trade. For a given manager the boundaries may be dictated by geography (U.S. companies only), company size (only companies above a certain value), or sector (energy companies but not technology firms). In all of these examples, the purpose of the constraint is to limit the investor to a universe of assets where they realistically believe they have an advantage over other portfolio managers. Warren Buffett used to admonish investors, "invest in what you know." The flip side of this advice is, avoid what you don't.

Markets are competitive. This competitive environment makes professional investing, in which a manager is attempting to outperform an index, a zero-sum game. The incremental dollar of additional profit that an investor produces comes out of someone else's pocket. It is worth contemplating this environment, one characterized by increasingly large, well-informed, and process-driven investors. All of whom are looking to profit by their superior knowledge at the expense of less-informed, less-scientific, and less-disciplined competitors. Given these disparities in resources and experience, the challenge of adding incremental returns through stock selection becomes quite apparent. It is worth remembering the geologist, meteorologist, and oncologist every time you think about taking a punt on a particular stock—do you know what they do?

THE PROBLEM WITH ACTIVE MUTUAL FUNDS

The previous section argued against individual investing in stocks directly. If professionals are better staffed and more disciplined, perhaps they can add incremental returns to your portfolio. If stock selection is too competitive, is it better to simply turn your investment decisions over to a professional? In answering this question, it is not enough to determine if a given manager can beat the market. The key questions are more subtle. First, can professional money managers add incremental returns, above the market's return, after their fees and expenses are accounted for? Second, how does the successful manager produce those returns? Third, if you can't pick the winning stocks, can you at least pick the winning managers?

The record of active mutual funds (those that try to beat an index rather than just replicate it) is not encouraging. Virtually all studies of mutual fund performance suggest that traditional active funds fail to add value once fees are accounted for. From 1994 through 2004, the S&P 500 returned 10.6 percent. In comparison, the average mutual fund returned less than 9 percent.[14] This underperformance was not driven by the market volatility that ensued when the bubble burst. In the ten years up to 1999, index funds returned an annual average of 14.7 percent to their investors, whereas actively managed funds returned 10.9 percent.[15] A longer-term look back yields similar results. Between 1984 and 2002, the return on the S&P 500 was 12.9 percent per year, according to Dalbar, a mutual fund research firm. Over the same period the average equity mutual fund returned 9.6 percent per year.[16]

This pattern of underperformance did not vary based on time frames or type of fund. During the thirty years since 1970, active managers of general U.S. stock funds failed to outperform the Wilshire 5000 index in seven out of ten years.[17] Even looking at longer-term holding periods did not improve the results. Over the past fifteen years, 82 percent of all active large-capitalization managers failed to beat their benchmark, the S&P 500.[18] Perhaps fund managers who focus on other markets fare better. Large-cap U.S. stock markets are notoriously efficient, meaning that information is so well disseminated that it is incredibly difficult to gain an advantage over other investors. However, not all markets are equally efficient. Some stock markets garner less attention from analysts and other investors, and as a result are perceived to be less efficient, or easier to beat. If this is the case, fund managers should have an easier time outperforming indices of smaller companies or markets outside the United States.

When we look at the record of fund managers who focus on either smaller U.S. companies or international ones, the story is the same. Poor performance is not unique to active U.S. large-cap fund managers. Those fund managers who focused on international securities or smaller U.S. companies also performed poorly. During the fifteen-year period to December 31, 2000, managers of foreign and U.S. small company stocks underperformed the MSCI EAFE index (large international stocks) and Ibbotson Small Company Index by 0.9 percent and 1.7 percent respectively.[19] Regardless of the time frame, markets involved, or methodology, fund managers, on average, tend to significantly trail the benchmark indices they are paid to beat. While there are years when fund managers do manage to add value, and the majority of managers actually beat their benchmarks, these are the exception rather than the rule. Even a cursory glance at the data suggests that the mutual fund industry has failed to deliver incremental, after-fee returns to their investors.

As depressing as these statistics are, the reality is actually a bit worse. Fund studies generally focus on existing funds, and do not include the performance of funds that have been closed or discontinued due to poor performance, a phenomenon known as "survivorship bias." Most experts agree that survivorship bias has the effect of flattering the performance of mutual funds, as the worst performers are generally excluded from the performance results. One study illustrates the point. From 1986 to 2000, active stocks managers in the United States trailed their respective benchmarks between 1.5 percent and 4.5 percent annually. However, if these numbers actually reflected the performance of funds that had been liquidated, the underperformance would be more dramatic. A paper published in *The Journal of Finance,* using Lipper data, suggests that active management returns are up to 1.4 percent per year lower when poor-performance or "dead funds" are included in the calculation.[20]

Thus far, I have limited the discussion to the traditional mutual fund industry, and have neglected the performance of hedge funds. Hedge funds are different from traditional mutual funds, which are registered with the SEC under the 1940 Investment Company Act.

In contrast, hedge funds are organized as private placements open only to sophisticated investors, generally taken to be institutional investors or wealthy individuals. In addition to the different legal structure, hedge funds have another important distinction from ordinary mutual funds: they can go short as well as long. As discussed in the last chapter, the ability to go short provides for significant improvements in the overall efficiency of a portfolio. Many hedge funds also take advantage of even more exotic financial instruments and techniques, such as complex derivative instruments. In short, they have a much wider array of financial tools at their disposal than typical long-only funds.

The evidence for hedge fund performance is murky, largely because of the difficulty in assembling the data. Hedge fund databases, even more than mutual fund data, suffer from survivorship bias, where the worst-performing hedge funds close, and subsequently are not included in the data. This has the impact of raising the average returns of the funds, and in the case of hedge funds by a potentially large margin. A recent study by Tremont Capital Management suggests that much of the vaunted outperformance of hedge funds disappears when correcting for these biases, some of which involve the ability of hedge fund managers to report their returns on a voluntary basis, which allows them to start the clock running only when they are pleased with their performance. Tricks like these, coupled with the survivorship bias, suggest that hedge fund returns may be vastly overstated. For example, the most famous hedge fund meltdown was the disintegration of Long-Term Capital Management in 1998. The firm, founded by former Salomon Brother stars, lost 92 percent of its capital from October 1997 to October 1998, but never reported the losses to database providers.[21]

An upward bias in hedge fund returns would put an enormous dent in the asset class's relative attractiveness. This is because lower average returns would be even harder to justify in light of the industry's outsized fees. A study of hedge fund returns suggests that if you adjust the returns of funds downward to account for the survivorship bias, the net return to investors begins to dissipate. The study's author lowered the assumed return on hedge funds from the 10.6 percent in the database to 8.6 percent. The change in assumptions made the asset class much less compelling when fees were calculated into the mix. In fact, assuming a standard 2-and-20 fee schedule— 2 percent management fee and 20 percent of the profits—the study questioned whether investors should be allocating any capital to hedge funds.[22] It is not that the funds could not beat the market, but rather that the benefits were accruing to the managers rather than the investors.

WHY DO MANAGERS UNDERPERFORM?

The above statistics seem a raw contradiction to the first part of the chapter. After all, aren't professional money managers better informed, more disciplined, and just plain smarter? Given all the advantages, what accounts for this collective failure on the part of institutional fund managers? It is not lack of skill or resources, but rather a function of two immutable laws of finance. First, by definition, most investors cannot outperform the average, and second, index performance does not take into account transaction costs, which real-world fund managers must incur. Before costs, the return on the average actively managed dollar will equal the return on the average passively managed dollar. In other words, in a world without trading costs or frictions, the average portfolio manager's return would equal the index. However, once transaction costs are taken into account, the return on the average actively managed dollar will be less than the return on the average passively managed dollar. Properly measured, the average actively managed dollar *must* underperform the average passively managed dollar.[23] The reality of trading with commissions, slippage, and bid/ask spreads guarantees that the average manager will underperform the index. The main culprit is not the incompetence of the industry, but the fact that most managers are collectively attempting to beat a benchmark. As the benchmark's performance is driven by these same managers, by definition, the majority of them cannot win.

The impact of transaction costs on performance is far from trivial given the average turnover of a typical fund manager. On average, a fund manager of an active U.S. stock fund turns his or her portfolio over 120 percent per year (the sum of the buys and sells compared to the assets in the fund). This compares to just 4 percent to 9 percent for a typical index manager.[24] The reason the latter category of managers trades so infrequently is that index managers are not making buy and sell decisions based on securities they believe will outperform the benchmark. Instead, they are simply trying to mimic the returns on their benchmark index by replicating the holdings of the index within their portfolio. Their trading is limited to those instances when the constituents of an index change and new securities have to be added to the portfolio, or others are removed.

In contrast, active managers, ones who are trying to beat rather than mimic an index, are frequently trading their portfolios as their opinions of market conditions change. Stocks that have gone up too much may be sold, while others that have gone down considerably now appear to be bargains. In this constant quest for finding securities that can produce above-benchmark returns, the money manager is incurring trading costs in the form of commissions, spreads, and market impact. The latter cost is a particular problem for most large fund managers. For individual investors buying 100, 500, or even 1,000 shares, there is normally sufficient liquidity in the market to accommodate the order. But consider the logistics of placing an order for 100,000 shares, something many large fund managers need to do on a regular basis. The very act of trying to purchase that many shares within a relatively short time frame drives the price against the managers, higher for those wishing to buy and lower for those wishing to sell. As trading costs can be significant, they create an additional hurdle for larger firms trying to outperform. There is another drag on performance related to actively managed mutual funds—the costs of running the fund itself. As highlighted in the previous chapter, all of the information advantages of institutional money managers come at a price, often a very steep price. Consulting oncologists do not come cheap, and even out-of-work meteorologists have learned their value to the industry, not to mention the costs of all of those computers to keep the quant models humming. The impact of a firm's fee structure on its after-fee performance has actually been studied, and the results are revealing. Underperformance by institutional managers is not a random pattern, but is largely influenced by the cost structure of the fund. The higher the fund manager's costs, the lower the likelihood he or she will actually beat the market. High-fee managers returned the lowest net performance, while those fund managers with the lowest cost structure produced the highest returns. It is not that fund managers cannot outperform the market, but that the costs associated with that outperformance (research, infrastructure, etc.) tend to neutralize the benefits to the shareholders of that fund.[25] These fees can be quite large, and represent a significant drag on the investor. Retail investors pay fees to portfolio managers (e.g., mutual fund groups) that can range from 0.7 percent to 3.1 percent annually. On average, the expense ratios are more than 1.6 percent per year.[26] Given the small differentials that separate beating the market from underperforming, an outlay of 1.6 percent per year is a large hurdle to overcome, making it understandable why most fund managers fail to deliver return-enhancing performance. When the incremental fees are added to the incremental trading costs, it is not surprising that most managers fail to add value—their costs are just too high.

CAN YOU PICK WINNING MANAGERS?

If the nature of the mutual fund industry prevents most managers from outperforming their benchmark or delivering superior after-fee performance, there is still the tantalizing possibility that at least a few managers can consistently deliver above-average returns. Are some managers just better than others? If this were the case, then an investor who could isolate the strong fund managers could improve his or her performance through the judicious selection of particular funds. While this is an appealing strategy, and the source of a cottage industry of fund ranking tables and business periodical headlines, it appears also to be a bit of an illusion. To the extent history is any guide, selecting winning managers is no easier than picking winning stocks. Virtually all studies of manager selection suggest that not only are individuals unable to pick above-average managers, but in the course of trying they actually make matters worse. This is because most investors select managers based on past performance; in other words, they tend to focus on the managers who have the best historical track record. By all accounts, this is exactly the wrong thing to do. By chasing performance, investors tend to rotate into managers at exactly the wrong time. Individual investors detract from their performance by switching to perceived winners. The evidence suggests that strong performance by fund managers does not last.

Between 1984 and 2002, passive investors who purchased an index fund and remained in it generated returns of approximately 13 percent per year. In contrast, those who placed their money with active fund managers generated less than 3 percent.[27] This awful performance is not simply a function of money managers' under-performing their benchmark. While the professionals may have trailed their benchmark by 1 percent to 3 percent per year, the bigger drag was the incessant switching of funds by retail investors. By always chasing last year's winners, investors tended to generate excessive transaction costs, as in many cases there is a significant sales or purchase fee associated with the funds they were buying and selling. They further compounded the problem by generally switching funds at the exact moment when a winning manager's streak was coming to an end.

A similar study by *Forbes* magazine demonstrated the same pattern. For many years, *Forbes* has been compiling and publishing a list of the best-performing mutual funds. The top performers are placed on the *Forbes* Honor Roll list. The top funds did indeed add incremental value during the period of their strong performance. For example, starting with the first five-year period, had an investor had perfect foresight and purchased the top thirty funds from 1970 to 1974, he or she would have outperformed the S&P 500 by 3.1 percent. However, those same funds that led their peers during that period trailed over the following twenty-five years. The top thirty funds from 1970 to 1974 underperformed the S&P 500 by 1.6 percent per year over the following twenty-five years.[28]

The reasons yesterday's winners turn into tomorrow's losers is not difficult to understand. It is not that managers lose their edge, but rather that the style and methods they employ may be applicable to one type of market, but less effective when market conditions change. Consider a fund manager who focuses on value stocks. The manager is searching for companies trading at some discount to their intrinsic value. A manager who followed this discipline would have generally outperformed in the period since the tech bubble burst in 2000. However, during the previous five years, when investors were focused on earnings growth, or more accurately potential earnings growth, that manager is likely to have underperformed. The reason is that during the immediate period leading up to the bursting of the tech bubble, growth stocks were routinely beating value stocks. In 2000, if an investor selected new mutual fund managers on the basis of their one-year track record, they are likely to have had too many growth managers and not enough value managers. Over the subsequent five years, this would have been exactly the wrong approach, as the bull market ended and investors refocused on valuations.

The lesson is that even the most skilled stock picker relies on methods and biases that are more effective under certain market conditions than under others. As those conditions change, the efficacy of that methodology will wax and wane. It is therefore very difficult to select winning managers, as it is to find winning stocks. This is particularly true given that most people pick managers on the basis of their recent performance. This approach tells you more about which investment styles are working than it does about which managers have actual talent. The extent to which market conditions, or, as they are known in the industry, "style biases," drive markets, is the topic of the next chapter.

Chapter 3

ALPHA AND BETA:
SEPARATING SKILL FROM RISK

The purpose of the previous two chapters was to outline the scope and breadth of the challenges facing individual investors. Markets are generally less benign than our experience of the last several decades would lead us to believe. In those instances where investors have attempted to add to their returns through stock selection, the results have been uninspiring. Nor are the challenges limited solely to the province of the individual investor. Large institutional investors have also demonstrated an inability to add enough incremental value to justify their fees and cost structure. These are the realities of modern-day investing. While it is natural to dream that we will have successive years of double-digit returns obtained without risk, the history of financial markets suggests otherwise.

Given these challenges, the best solution for an individual investor is to assemble a low-cost and well-diversified portfolio. As discussed in chapter 1, markets don't normally rise forever, and often go down as well as up. A portfolio with exposure to many markets helps to mitigate the damage when this occurs. At the same time, if professionals are not adding value, then avoid paying big fees, which only serve to enrich them and lower your returns. If individuals can't beat the market, and professionals rarely add enough return to justify their fees, the key for the individual is to own a diversified portfolio of different markets and assets at the cheapest possible price. While minimizing fees is fairly obvious, the benefits of diversification are more subtle, but equally important. A diversified portfolio will help ensure that your portfolio produces the maximum return for a given level of risk. Avoiding active mutual funds will minimize the cost of gaining access to those markets, as well as the risk of chasing yesterday's returns in hopes of finding tomorrow's winners.

In order to build the portfolio described above, it is worth one more digression to gain a better understanding of what diversification really is, and why it is beneficial. In the course of this analysis, it will also become obvious why risk and return are so intertwined. As the remainder of the book will focus on the various building blocks of a diversified portfolio, it will be helpful to obtain a solid grounding in exactly what we are speaking about. What does it mean to have exposure to a market, or to have different betas in a portfolio? Why are some combinations of investments better than others? Almost all individual investors think of a portfolio as a collection of stocks, bonds, and perhaps mutual funds. In other words, they think of the assets that are assembled in their brokerage account. The purpose of this chapter is to facilitate a shift in how you think of your portfolio. Rather than contemplating the assets, it will often be useful to consider what those assets represent. What risks do those assets (small-cap returns, growth stocks, commodities, etc.) expose you to, and what are the returns associated with those risks? The difference in perspective will make the latter part of the book, how to assemble a portfolio of exchange traded funds, feel more intuitive.

In order to build that theoretical grounding, we will introduce several of the cornerstone theories of modern finance. In particular, we will see the importance of making an accurate estimation of overall market returns for forecasting the return on an individual portfolio. Second, modern financial theory will illustrate why selecting individual securities without an informational edge is only likely to produce incremental risk without any corresponding benefit in returns. The notion of risk, discussed briefly in previous sections, will be treated to a more formal discussion. In order to understand the benefit of risk-adjusted return and diversification, it is critical to first have a solid grounding in what risk actually is, and how it relates to return.

Chapter 2 spent a good deal of time delving into the topic of returns above a benchmark. Up to this point, I have used a fairly informal definition of excess returns. Before proceeding it is worth establishing a more formal definition. In previous chapters we mentioned the necessity of adjusting the return of an asset by factoring in the asset's risk. Another adjustment is to control for the amount of return you could get on a riskless asset, normally measured as the annual return on a Treasury bill. The logic behind this calculation is that a risky asset should produce higher returns than an asset whose return is guaranteed (why would anyone risk money on stocks if they expected to earn the same return as they could get on a CD or money market account?). By subtracting out the risk-free rate, you are left with a measure of return that can be better related to the risk characteristics of a stock or other risky asset. In describing the theoretical relationship between an asset's specific characteristics and its returns, I will draw on two key theories of modern finance, the Capital Asset Pricing Model, or CAPM, and the Arbitrage Pricing Theory, or APT. Together, these two theories will help to frame the notion of *alpha/beta separation*, a concept that is increasingly critical for professional investors, and one that will help establish the justification for investing in exchange traded funds.

THE CAPITAL ASSET PRICING MODEL: ALPHA VERSUS BETA

Risk has different meanings in finance. On a very visceral level, traders simply view risk as the amount of money they stand to lose. Back during the financial crisis of 1998, risk was manifested by a computer screen showing sellers and no buyers. Under more normal conditions, risk is often described as the volatility of a stock. This leaves the question of how to define *volatility*. One way to define it is to measure the standard deviation of returns. The standard deviation is a statistical tool that quantifies the dispersion of a set of numbers around an average, or as it is known in statistical parlance, the mean. An average measures the central tendency of data. In contrast, the standard deviation measures how much the data is spread around that average. The larger the standard deviation, the more volatility in the data set. Stocks or portfolios with high standard deviations tend to be very volatile, with a wide dispersion of returns.

Think of two portfolios. The first portfolio returns 1 percent per month, the second goes up 4 percent every other month, but loses 2 percent on the off month. For the sake of simplicity, let's ignore the impact of compounding, and say that both portfolios return approximately 12 percent per year or 1 percent a month on average (in actuality, the portfolio that returns 1 percent a month actually does slightly better). The first portfolio, the one that gains 1 percent per month, has a standard deviation of zero. All of the monthly returns are the same as the average. In contrast, the portfolio that goes up and down has a standard deviation of more than 3 percent. It is the more volatile of the two as monthly returns tend to deviate from that average. Both portfolios produce monthly returns of 1 percent, but the second portfolio's returns tend to fluctuate widely around that average. The fluctuations, or volatility, are measured by the standard deviation of the returns.

Besides illustrating the notion of standard deviations, the previous example brings home another point: of these two portfolios, which one would you rather own? In both cases your return is approximately the same. However, the second portfolio is more likely to generate a bit of anxiety. If you're going to make the same amount of money, why not make it with less worry? Stocks that fluctuate violently in value should also offer the potential of more upside than less volatile assets. As the example illustrates, the relationship between risk and return is ultimately grounded in human psychology rather than statistics or financial theory. Most investors will demand to be compensated for the risk of losing money. The more they stand to lose, another potential measure of risk, the more they expect to get paid. This is why more volatile stocks should have higher expected returns, in order to compensate investors for the risk of owning them.

Interestingly, while the trade-off between risk and reward is an intuitive notion, it was not until Harry Markowitz first introduced the concept of the "efficient frontier" in 1952 that modern financial theory became established. It was Markowitz who first quantified the mathematical relationships necessary to find the optimal portfolio for a given level of risk (i.e., the portfolio that would produce the highest-level return). A portfolio is considered efficient in Markowitz's framework if it has minimum risk among all portfolios with the same expected return.[1] One of the powerful implications of this discovery is that it allows you to look at the problem of risk and reward from either direction. In other words, the math works both ways—you can find a portfolio that maximizes return for a given level of risk, or a portfolio that minimizes risk for a given return. Either way, you have a mathematical tool box for finding the optimal portfolio.

Markowitz employed the notion of standard deviation as a measure of risk. There is also a second way to define risk that is commonly employed in modern finance. This method relies on comparing the returns of a stock or portfolio to the returns of something else, normally a benchmark index such as the S&P 500. If the benchmark represents the market, this measure of risk quantifies the volatility of a stock relative to the volatility of the market. This measure, the relative risk of a security, is most frequently known as *beta*. Beta is one of the key ingredients of the CAPM. The model suggests that the return on a stock, or portfolio of stocks, is a function of three variables: the risk-free rate of return, representing the return an investor could get on a riskless asset; the return of the overall stock market; and the beta of the stock. The logic behind the CAPM's assertion is fairly simple. The CAPM states that investors

are compensated for taking necessary risks, but not for taking unnecessary risks. Risk in the market portfolio is necessary and ines-
capable, but residual risk (the risk that is specific to a given security)
is self-imposed. One consequence of this is that investors who don't
think they have superior information on a stock should own the
market portfolio, that is, an index.[2]

The CAPM suggests that you can separate the risk or volatility
associated with a stock into two components: a market component,
which you cannot escape, and a stock-specific component. The
market component of risk cannot be avoided—if you're in the
market, you will have risk. The good news is that generally you're
compensated for that risk; that is, stocks produce higher returns
than does sticking your money under the mattress or even in a
bank account. But there is a second component as well—the risk
that is idiosyncratic to a specific security (e.g., if you buy an energy
stock, there is common risk to the market and energy prices,
but there is also stock-specific risk in the sense that the company's next exploration may well come up dry). What the CAPM implies, and investors need to remember, is that the market will not
necessarily compensate you for the idiosyncratic risks of owning a
particular stock. The reason is that the risks associated with any individual stock are avoidable. You can mitigate the risk by owning a
bunch of stocks with different characteristics, or even better you can
fully avoid the specific risks of a particular stock by owning the entire market, in other words, a market index. So according to the
CAPM, if you don't have insights into a particular stock, own a diversified basket of securities. If you happen to know that the aforementioned oil company's next well will be a gusher, by all means
buy the stock. But in the absence of any specific insights, avoid the

risk. Otherwise, you're accepting marginal risk for which you are not being compensated.

In the context of this theory, the market portfolio is assumed to be some metaportfolio encompassing all assets (although in practice we normally use a much narrower benchmark, such as the S&P 500). There is no way to avoid the risk of the market, but we can avoid the idiosyncratic risks of a given security by diversifying our portfolios. Diversification balances out the risks of one type of security with those of another. If the securities are sufficiently different, they are unlikely to move together, thereby lowering the volatility on the overall portfolio. If you have fifty well-diversified stocks in your portfolio, the differing performances will prevent your portfolio from moving too dramatically at any one time. In those instances when it does, it is because the overall market is moving violently. This risk is unavoidable if you have any exposure to the market, but per the CAPM, you can avoid the risks of any one stock through diversification. Taken to its logical extreme, the best diversification is obtained by owning the broadest possible portfolio, that is, the market portfolio. In this instance, you have now diversified away all the idiosyncratic risk of individual stocks or other assets.

Central to the CAPM are two different assertions. First, there is the notion of a market portfolio that theoretically represents the entire universe of investment assets. Obviously, this is a bit of a simplifying assumption, as no index could ever represent all the different assets in the world: stocks, bonds, commodities, real estate. . . . Most investors who utilize the CAPM just use a generic market index, such as the Wilshire 5000, as a proxy for the market. The second concept behind the CAPM is the notion of beta, which provides a link on how a particular stock or portfolio will perform when compared to this benchmark or index. When comparing the return on the market versus the return on the portfolio, the theory actually focuses on what is known as excess return, which I mentioned at the beginning of the chapter. Excess return is formally defined as the market return minus the return on the risk-free asset—in effect quantifying how much the market is paying you for owning a risky asset. Again, risky assets should pay more than less risky assets. Using excess return, beta is mathematically equal to the covariance of the portfolio divided by the variance of the market. The market portfolio, or index, is assumed to have a beta of one (which is just a fancy way of saying if you buy the market, you will get the market return), while the risk-free rate has a beta of zero (if you buy a Treasury bill, you will get the same return regardless of what the market does as there is no risk).[3] To return to the mathematics for a moment, covariance is another statistical metric that relates the co-movement of two sets of numbers. A high, positive covariance indicates that two sets of data move together in tandem, while a negative covariance would mean that the two move in opposite directions. The variance is simply the square of the standard deviation discussed previously. In English, this means that beta is mathematically dependent on the extent to which the security and market co-move as well as the volatility of the market itself. The more the market and a particular security move together, the higher their covariance, and the higher the beta. The key point to take from all of this is that beta is a very efficient way to link the returns on a stock to the returns on the overall market. The CAPM simplifies previous work in portfolio construction. The gist of the model is that portfolio returns can be divided into two components: a beta component, which represents the systematic risk of the portfolio, and an alpha component, which is linked to the specific risk of the individual securities.[4] One implication of this theory is that, assuming your portfolio is already diversified, the more you risk, the higher your expected returns.

There is another implication to the CAPM—when markets are in equilibrium, specific risks associated with individual securities can be diversified away, leaving investors with just the market risk, beta.[5] We've tossed the term out quite a bit, but within the context of this theory, diversification has a very specific meaning. In portfolio construction, you build diversified portfolios by combining assets with a low to negative correlation—in other words, assets whose returns tend to be independent of each other. Correlation is another statistical measurement, closely related to covariance and standard deviation. Correlation is actually just a normalized version of covariance, in that it has a scale. All correlations are between negative 1 and positive 1. A correlation of 1 indicates perfect co-movement between two sets of data, while a correlation of negative 1 indicates that they are inversely related (one goes up proportionally whenever the other goes down). Correlations of zero indicate absolutely no relationship between the two variables. The value of the CAPM is that it provides an intellectual framework for deconstructing the returns produced by a fund manager—something that will be very valuable when it comes time to decide if that fund manager is overcharging you. In other words, are the returns he or she is generating simply a function of risk, rather than skill? The CAPM allows you to try to answer that question.

If a stock's returns are generally equal to the market's returns it has a beta of one, which is the market's beta. Stocks that are traditionally more volatile than the market have a beta higher than one. This implies that their returns are likely to be a multiple of those produced by the broader market, or benchmark. Finally, stocks that generally display less risk than the overall market have betas less than one. These stocks are considered more defensive, in that they are likely to go down less than the market during periods of financial turbulence. The flip side is that the low-beta or defensive stocks are likely to appreciate less than the market during rallies. It is theoretically possible to have a security with a negative beta. In other words, the stock would appreciate when the rest of the market is moving down. An actual example of this would have been gold stocks during certain periods.

Returns associated with beta are not a free lunch. If you have a stock that produces excess returns of 20 percent in a year when the market's return is 10 percent, this does not necessarily suggest that you are a brilliant stock picker. It is very likely that the stock went up because its beta is higher than one. The downside of such a stock is, if next year the market goes down by 10 percent your investment is likely to decline by more than the market. This is a critical point for individual investors. When assessing anyone's purported market skill, especially your own, you must adjust for the overall risk of the security or portfolio you are evaluating. Returns derived from beta are a function of risk rather than the ability to select good stocks. This is why quants try to maximize risk-adjusted returns rather than just returns. To maximize returns, all an investor needs to do is increase the beta of his or her portfolio. However, those higher returns are coming with the very real possibility of losing more money. Remember, skill commands higher fees, but managers who produce returns by increased risk, beta, do not. When presented with an advertisement for a market-beating fund manager, the first question to ask is, how much risk did he or she take in order to outperform?

There are other implications to the CAPM that are also worth considering. The CAPM postulates that the expected excess residual return, or alpha, on stocks or a portfolio is zero.[6] If the residual return is zero, then the return on any security or on a portfolio is determined by two factors, the return on the market and the beta of the security or portfolio. If the CAPM is to be believed, the return an investor should expect on his or her portfolio is a function of how the market does (the reason for the lengthy digression in chapter 1) and the risk of an investor's portfolio.

As the return on the market is beyond the control of any investor, according to the CAPM the only lever available to affect returns is the amount of risk an investor chooses to accept. The more risk you take—that is, market risk—the higher your expected return should be. If you build a portfolio with a beta considerably higher than the market, you will earn more during good times and lose more during bad times. And while there may be discrepancies from year to year, a higher-risk portfolio can reasonably be assumed to earn a higher return over a prolonged, multidecade time frame. Conversely, if you are naturally risk averse, the simplest solution is to construct a portfolio with a below-market beta. While you will probably trail the market during advances, you will not suffer the same volatility when market conditions worsen. In a quest for higher returns, investors should assume that they are also implicitly accepting higher risk. Unfortunately, this is not what most investors have in mind when they are seeking to enhance the returns of their portfolio.

As mentioned previously, investors are compensated in the form of higher returns for taking additional risk, but they are not compensated for taking unnecessary risk. Market risk is unavoidable, but security-specific risk can be negated by constructing a well-diversified portfolio. So if you are taking security-specific risk, the market will not compensate you. In this case, you are on your own. If you choose not to diversify and have a concentrated portfolio, you are accepting additional risk for which you are not likely to be compensated. In the absence of security-specific information, you should avoid stock picking. Under the CAPM, an individual whose portfolio differs from the market is playing a zero-sum game. The player has additional risk and no additional expected return.[7] Based on the discussion in chapter 2, it is worth considering whether you really have enough information to justify the incremental risk of buying a specific security.

ARBITRAGE PRICING THEORY: BETAS ABOUND

There is a second theory on the link between portfolio returns and risks that also merits an introduction. This theory is known as the Arbitrage Pricing Theory, or APT. The APT was developed in 1976 by Stephen Ross. Both the CAPM and APT agree that company-specific factors influence stock prices, but that these risks can be canceled out in a well-diversified portfolio. The APT argues that even in well-diversified portfolios, there are still residual risks due to common factors and economic forces that impact the overall market. The primary difference between the APT and CAPM is that while the CAPM posits just one source of risk, the market risk, the APT accepts different sources of risk. The theory does not specify what the sources are or how to enumerate them. Investors employing the APT typically focus on economic factors such as interest rates, inflation, and business activity.[8] However, while economic forces are typically used in the APT, it is worth highlighting that they need not be the only, or even primary, factors. Other noneconomic sources of risk could be investor sentiment, commodity exposure, or geopolitical risk. The APT is a general theory in that it does not specify what the factors are. Unlike the CAPM, which posits a single source of risk, the APT allows for many sources. Whether one source of risk or many, both theories maintain that the return on your portfolio is a function of the return on the various risk factors and the degree to which your portfolio is leveraged to those risk factors. In moving from the CAPM to the APT, think in terms of multiple betas, covering all types of different risks, rather than just one.

While there is only one factor exposure in the CAPM, market risk, and there can be multiple ones in the APT, both models rely on quantifying a stock or portfolio's exposure to the factors through the concept of beta. The APT states that each stock's expected excess return is determined by the stock's factor exposures. For each factor there is a weight. Any stock or portfolio's expected return is the sum over all the factors of the stock's factor exposures times the factor returns. The theory does not state what the factors are, how to calculate a stock's exposure to the factors, or what the weights should be in the linear combination. While this seems of limited use, it is actually quite valuable. The APT offers an intellectually flexible framework to understand security returns. The theory's flexibility is one of its advantages, as it allows analysts to explore how different forces can affect the performance of any portfolio.

There are periods when the CAPM, and its singular approach to risk, are inadequate to describe a stock's returns (by singular, I mean that there is only one key measure of risk, beta, to the market). The APT addresses this shortcoming by allowing for more than one source of return.[9] In providing for this greater flexibility, the APT forces investors to think about additional sources of return, rather than just the market. There may be other types of betas that an investor needs to consider. The theoretical under-pinnings of the APT helped pave the way for the multiple factor risk model that has become a staple of quantitative portfolio man-agement. The risk model is based on the concept that the return of any stock can be expressed by a collection of common factors, plus an idiosyncratic component that is particular to that security.[10] The common factors can explain much of the variation in the secu-rities' return. These factors need to be broad enough to encompass most of the forces that impact stock performance. The list includes everything from a stock's industry classification to its value characteristics.

Take for example the energy stock discussed earlier. Using the CAPM, all of the stock's common risk comes from the market. But we also know that energy stocks are highly influenced by energy prices. As the price of oil or natural gas rises, so do these stocks. So the APT would allow for a second beta. Under this formula, the ex-cess return on the stock would be a function not only of the market, but also of the price of crude oil. In this instance, the flexibility of the APT would probably provide for a better description of the stock's return than the CAPM, which just posits the one source of common risk.

The justification for the risk model is to disaggregate the sources

---

CAPM and APT

- Both models quantify the risk of a security according to its sensitivity to other factors. The sensitivity to a particular factor is quantified by the Greek letter β, beta.
- CAPM posits one source of risk, the market risk, and relates a stock's risk to that of the overall market. The higher the beta, the more risky the security.
- APT assumes multiple sources of risk. While these risks are not specified, they can encompass any factor that theoretically drives market returns. The factors are often interpreted to be macroeconomic in nature. According to the APT, a stock's risk is the sum of its sensitivities to these various risk factors.

---

of return into different buckets. Each stock has different attributes across different dimensions. The dimensions include the type of company (industry classification), value characteristics (how cheap or expensive the stock is versus its peers), the volatility of its earnings, or even its recent performance (momentum). At different times, investors value different characteristics or attributes, and as the investor's appetite for different characteristics changes, so do the returns associated with those characteristics. When investors had a preference for growth stocks during the late 1990s, any security with that attribute performed well. The more the stock was leveraged to that theme, in other words the higher the stock's beta to growth, the better it was likely to perform. Perhaps the stock was also a technology company. Now, in addition to the attribute of growth, it also benefited from the market's appetite for technology shares. Continuing this process of decomposing across multiple dimensions, we can explain a good deal of a stock's performance. The key is to know the returns on the different factors, and to be able to quantify a security's beta, or sensitivity, to those factors.

This approach to markets is a useful construct for individual investors as well as professional quants. Individuals may not have the tools or the need to build elaborate mathematical models. But even without the math, the concept of portfolios as a collection of betas is a very useful mental framework. When considering building a portfolio, rather than thinking in terms of stocks, think in terms of the risk exposures. What exposures do you want, and how do you combine different exposures in a manner that maximizes your risk-adjusted return? As described above, the betas can represent everything from value stocks, to particular industries, to characteristics such as volatility or financial leverage.

So in building your portfolio, how should you go about gaining exposure to different risk factors? If you believe that health care is a good long-term bet, you want to gain direct exposure to the risk factor of "health care." In doing so, you are better off purchasing an asset that provides direct beta to that risk factor rather than an individual drug stock that carries idiosyncratic risk you may not want. If what you really want in your health-care beta is a play on an aging populace and advancing medical technology, why dilute the beta of the industry with the idiosyncratic risk of a particular drug company? A pharmaceutical company's stock is likely to vacillate based on a number of factors, many of which are specific to the company. Did its latest blockbuster drug pass its most recent clinical test? Is there a pending lawsuit? None of these risks are what you originally intended when you wanted exposure to the health-care industry. Instead, you are now betting on the prospects of the company, about which you may know little. When thinking about beta or risk exposure, the goal is to gain the exposure to the correct risk factor while at the same time eliminating the idiosyncratic, stock-specific risk in your portfolio.

The second key point to remember is that beta is both cheap and easy to replicate. Thanks to the proliferation of different financial instruments, including exchange traded funds, most common risk factors, or betas, can be obtained without paying a professional manager an active fee. In fact, betas by definition imply a common risk factor that is not correlated with the stock-specific returns, or alpha, that are idiosyncratic to particular securities. Beta is cheap, and anyone who is trying to command premium fees for providing beta is profiting at your expense.

Take the simplest example of beta, leverage to the overall market. If an investor had a high tolerance for risk, let us say a young, financially secure professional who is saving for retirement, they could raise their expected return simply by increasing their portfolio's beta to the overall market. There are several ways to do this (emphasis on more volatile stocks, sectors, or countries, etc.). However, all the different approaches have one thing in common: they do not necessitate paying large fees to someone to seek higher returns. Returns can be generated through the manipulation of the portfolio's beta. If the market rises, the investor will be rewarded, just as they will suffer more severe losses if the market retreats. If all an investor wants from a portfolio manager is risk, they need not pay very much to replicate it.

Alpha is a different manner. Adding incremental return, without incremental risk, requires skill, and that skill comes at a much steeper price. Investment managers who can demonstrate alpha should command a higher premium for their services. This would seem to be a relatively straightforward matter. However, it becomes more complicated when you consider other risk factors beyond the market. How do you disentangle the returns? What part of the returns is associated with risk factors, and what part can be attributed to the skill of the manager? Without going through this exercise it will be difficult to assess what the manager's services were worth. If all the returns were generated through common risk factors, like a value bias, the manager does not merit a large fee. If, on the other hand, the manager was able to generate significant excess returns without exposure to common risk factors, then he or she may be worth the expense.

Historically, it was much more difficult to implement this approach, even if one was able to separate out the alpha and beta components of return. Up until recently there was a dearth of instruments providing exposure to cheap sources of beta. In the case of more esoteric factors, such as volatility or dividend yield, there may have been no financial instrument at all to provide the requisite exposure. At the very least, it would have been more costly to gain access to these types of factors. As financial markets have developed in recent years, this is no longer the case. An active mutual fund, which charges higher fees, is no longer necessary. In fact, in many cases, institutional fund manager returns can be demonstrated to be leveraged to a simple theme, like small-cap or value. While this may be a smart bet, an investor who pays active fees to make this bet is overpaying for the service. Maintaining a portfolio constantly leveraged to small-cap names can be accomplished at a fraction of the cost of a traditional mutual fund. This is what financial professionals are referring to when they speak about alpha/beta separation. They are attempting to separate the common risk factors in a portfolio from the components that require real skill in either security selection or market timing. As investors have become savvier in identifying different types of risk factors, the necessity to demonstrate real skill, rather than a particular investment bias, has increased. As we shall see in the second part of the book, ETFs are a particularly effective way to gain exposure to different risk factors in a cost-efficient manner. If all you want from a portfolio manager is a value bet, international exposure, or a preference for high-volatility stocks, there are now numerous products that can provide that exposure in an easy and cost-efficient manner.

While the first part of the book was intentionally designed to debunk myths and expose the multiple challenges facing investors, I would like to end it on a positive note. New financial products have made it both easier and cheaper to build a well-diversified portfolio. These innovations have also made it possible to gain exposure to a varied assortment of different risk factors that were previously difficult to replicate. The reason this is advantageous to investors is that many of these risk factors are sufficiently different as to offer real diversification benefits. As discussed above, by adding uncorrelated betas, you improve the risk-adjusted return on your portfolio. You in effect raise the expected return on the portfolio for a given level of risk. Diversification is as close to a free lunch as you can get in investing. Investors want to take the maximum benefit from this relationship by assembling a sufficiently diversified portfolio. The more diversified the better. Unlike the challenges described in chapter 2, which involved the search for active alpha, the difficulties in assembling a diversified portfolio are more easily addressed. The goal is to focus on allocation to different assets in an effort to move toward a more efficient portfolio allocation, and by efficient I mean a portfolio that delivers higher risk-adjusted re-turns. These readily available allocation alphas serve a critical and valuable role in moving a portfolio toward optimal strategic alloca-tion.[11] It is to the search for these efficient allocations that we will now turn.

PART 2

SOLUTIONS

Chapter 4

INTRODUCTION TO EXCHANGE TRADED FUNDS

I n the first part of this book I focused on the challenges of finding cost-efficient alpha, either through individual stock selection or through professional money management. Having outlined the problem, in the remainder of the book I will look at one potential solution: using exchange traded funds (ETFs) as a tool for building a portfolio of cheap and well-diversified beta. This chapter will provide an introduction to exchange traded funds and address basic questions concerning these vehicles. The goal is to give an overview of the product from several perspectives, including size of the market, how ETFs are constructed, costs, trading nuances, and tax implications.

The ETF is similar to its older cousin the index fund in that it seeks to replicate the performance of an index of securities. Recent versions have gone beyond traditional indices, and now attempt to represent certain characteristics of a group of stocks, such as companies that generate a significant number of patents. Like an index fund, the ETF replicates the holdings of an index by holding securities in a proportional amount to the underlying index itself. If an index includes 3 percent of General Motors, an ETF seeking to replicate that index will also have 3 percent of its assets in General Motors. Unlike an active mutual fund that deviates from its benchmark in an attempt to outperform it, the goal of an index fund is simply to replicate the returns of that index by mimicking its holdings.

Where ETFs differ from index funds is in how they trade. Traditional mutual funds are bought and sold at a price consistent with the closing value of the fund on a given day. If you place an order to buy a fund, your order will be filled at the net asset value, or NAV, of the fund at the close of that trading day (the NAV is based on the value of all the securities within that fund). You cannot buy or sell a traditional mutual fund at an intraday price. In other words, the price you get will be the closing price, regardless of when you placed the order during the day. In contrast, exchange traded funds trade more like stocks, in that their price fluctuates throughout the trading day. Because ETFs trade like stocks, investors enjoy a flexibility that is not available with traditional mutual funds, either active or index. An ETF can be bought or sold with different types of orders, such as market and limit. In addition, an ETF can be purchased using leverage—on margin—or shorted (*leverage* refers to using money borrowed from your broker to purchase additional shares, while *shorting* is a technique by which you sell stock you do not own, betting it will go down in price). Unlike many active mutual funds, ETFs do not charge a commission to buy or sell, often referred to as a "load," although you will pay a brokerage commission. Another difference between the exchange traded fund and the traditional mutual fund is that the holdings of the ETF are transparent to investors. The manager, or sponsor, of the ETF provides a portfolio composition to the market every day.[1] So when you purchase an ETF, you are always aware of what stocks constitute your portfolio. In contrast, traditional mutual funds only have to release their holdings at certain regular intervals, creating some opacity over what stocks they are actually investing in.

THE DIFFERENT FLAVORS OF ETFs

Before proceeding too far in our introduction, it is worth clarifying exactly what an exchange traded fund is. While many investors, as well as the media, treat exchange traded funds as a monolith, different funds come in different flavors. Given that these flavors have implications for how the funds are managed, having a better understanding of the different structures is useful. In general, when issuers or sponsors create what have become known as exchange traded funds, they have several competing goals. First, they need an entity that can be publicly traded. Second, the entity needs to be exempt from tax at the corporate level (individuals pay taxes on income and capital gains from the fund, but the fund itself pays no tax). Depending upon the time the fund was created and the types of assets it was designed to hold, different sponsors have selected different types of vehicles with which to launch their funds. For example, recent funds based on commodities may have different structures from funds based on an index of equity securities. The difference in structure is a function of the fact that the instruments hold different types of assets—futures or commodities versus equity securities.

To date, there are several different types of funds, all of which are generally categorized as ETFs. Those flavors include the aforementioned open-ended mutual fund, exchange traded unit investment trusts, and exchange traded grantor trusts. While all three types are commonly referred to as ETFs, there are certain differences of which investors should be aware.

Let's start with the open-ended mutual fund. This type of fund is registered under the Investment Company Act of 1940 and uses the same structure as most traditional mutual funds. Funds in this category are allowed to use derivatives, and can generate income from security lending (i.e., allowing short sellers to borrow their securities in exchange for a fee). Dividends in these funds are reinvested in the fund on the day they are received, and then paid out on a quarterly basis. ETFs in this category include the Select Sector SPDRs and iShares.[2]

Exchange traded funds organized under the 1940 Act also have additional flexibility in the manner in which they replicate their exposure to the underlying index. While most ETFs in this category simply hold the underlying components of an index, a sponsor of this type of ETF can use sampling or optimization techniques.[3] This means that rather than holding all the stocks in a particular basket, an ETF set up as an open-ended fund can employ statistical tools that seek to mimic the performance of the index with a slightly different mix of securities. The advantage to this is that there may be a combination of stocks or other assets that provides an almost identical exposure to the index, but that is cheaper to trade.

The primary difference between an ETF and a traditional open-ended mutual fund is in how the fund handles redemptions. A traditional mutual fund provides daily liquidity to the investors based on the closing net asset value (NAV) for that day. The ability to redeem holdings on a daily basis for cash is a defining characteristic of open-ended funds. While ETFs are technically open-ended funds, they handle redemptions differently. An ETF need only provide daily redemptions to authorized participants, that is, large institutions, and then only in large blocks. The reason ETFs are able to restrict the terms of redemptions is that individual investors can sell their funds in real time on an exchange. It is this mechanism that provides liquidity for investors. Instead of selling your holdings back to a fund sponsor, as you would do with a traditional mutual fund, you sell your ETF on an exchange to another investor. In order to establish a new ETF, fund sponsors must apply to the SEC for a specific exemption to this provision of the 1940 Investment Company Act. It is this exemption to the normal mechanism for redeeming holdings that distinguishes exchange traded funds from traditional mutual funds.

The second type of structure utilized is the exchange traded unit investment trust. These funds are considered trusts, more specifically grantor trusts, for tax purposes and are therefore exempt from corporate taxes. In contrast to the first type of exchange traded fund, the UIT must replicate the holdings of the underlying index. In order to qualify for the trust status, these types of funds must replicate an index, and cannot manage the securities, or cash, in any manner. In other words, this structure demands a totally passive process in maintaining exposure to the target index. A second difference is that security lending is not allowed, removing a potential source of income for these funds. A third difference is that dividends are not reinvested in these funds, but are paid out quarterly in cash.[4]

Again, the paying out of the dividends, rather than reinvesting, is a necessary function of the trust status. Reinvestment of the dividends would be considered active management, which is not allowed under the trust status of the instrument. One other point concerning the unit investment trusts: there are instances where diversification rules within the 1940 Act can force these funds to deviate from the exact benchmark weights. The reason for this is that the 1940 Act stipulates that no fund can invest more than 25 percent of its assets in any single issuer. For nondiversified funds, the aggregate limit is 50 percent of the fund's total assets. This can be a problem as some small indices, particularly ones based on a single sector or industry, can have a large weight in a single stock. In these instances, several funds will use optimization tools to adjust their holdings to reflect the index weightings while still holding to the diversification rules.[5] Generally, this type of structure went out of fashion in the mid- to late 1990s. While several popular funds such as the QQQ, DIAMONDS, and S&P SPDRs, use this structure, virtually all stock-based funds launched over the past decade are organized as open-ended mutual funds with an SEC exemption for daily redemptions.

The third category of product included within the ETF penumbra is exchange traded grantor trusts. The difference between these instruments and the previous one is that while they are organized as grantor trusts for tax purposes, this type of instrument is not registered under the Investment Company Act.[6] While they are still registered with the SEC, they are regulated by the Division of Corporate Finance, which regulates ordinary shares. In contrast, funds registered under the 1940 Act are regulated by the Division of Investment Management. These instruments can be thought of as pools of securities, with receipts representing an underlying claim to a portion of that pool. What is unique about this type of structure is that the fund composition does not change over time, with the exception of adjustments to reflect corporate actions. This has the effect of making these funds static, and not subject to subsequent rebalancing. In other words, they do not evolve in their members and weights as would a fund based on an index, such as the S&P 500.

This grantor trust structure most closely resembles owning the underlying stocks. These funds can be redeemed for the underlying securities in the funds, and investors retain the voting rights on the underlying securities. Furthermore, as with the UIT, dividends are distributed directly to shareholders rather than reinvested. Investors are the beneficial owners of the underlying shares and thus directly receive dividends and company reports, and are responsible for voting the shares.[7] Finally, these funds do not charge a management fee or expense ratio (remember, as the holdings are static and dividends are paid out directly, there is nothing to "manage"). Instead, fund expenses are paid out of the fund's income—that is, dividends.

The best example of this type of fund is the HOLDRs, or holding company depository receipts. These funds use the grantor trust structure to create a static basket of securities, normally between twenty and fifty, which represent a particular market segment, normally an industry or sector. The composition of the HOLDR does not change after the issue, with the exception of a special case such as a merger and acquisition.[8] A drawback of this structure is that as the holdings remain constant over time, the instrument's representation of a given index or theme will shift over time. This is because the HOLDR is not rebalanced, but will maintain a static position in its underlying securities. As weightings change in an index, different stocks may gain a new dominance within that industry (think of the rise and fall of certain technology companies between the late 1990s and the early part of this decade). As the composition of the index shifts, but that of the HOLDRs does not, the instrument may not provide the same exposure to a given theme as it did when you originally purchased it.

There are other potential issues with the HOLDRs that investors should be aware of. While investors can directly redeem these funds for the underlying securities, the fund must be traded in round lots of 100 shares.[9] This may create issues for smaller investors. As the HOLDRs generally represent relatively narrow (i.e., not diversified) indices, an investor may not want to allocate a large portion of his or her portfolio to a particular HOLDR. For example, one of the most popular HOLDRs is the BBH, or U.S. Biotech HOLDR. During the summer of 2007, the fund was trading for somewhere around $80 a share. A hypothetical investor in the fund would need to be willing to invest at least $8,000 in this particular HOLDR. To increase their position in the fund, they would need to make subsequent investments of at least $8,000. Depending upon the size of an individual's portfolio, this could represent a relatively large allocation to a fairly narrow segment of the market. For the above reason, the HOLDRs may be more appropriate for larger investors who can afford to allocate a significant dollar amount to a particular industry or theme.

As the market for exchange traded funds expands, new mechanisms and new takes on old structures are proliferating. One of the drivers of this trend is the expansion of ETFs into other asset classes. As exchange traded funds move beyond stocks, new funds are likely to adopt different legal structures. One limitation on grantor trusts is that to gain the tax-exempt status, they cannot hold securities, although they can track an index of securities in an unmanaged process. As many of the new exchange traded funds are commodity based, the limitation on securities does not apply (commodities are not considered securities). There are several examples of these funds on the commodity side, including the streetTRACKS Gold Trust (GLD), iShares Silver Trust (SLV), as well as numerous funds based on currency baskets. In addition, some of the new commodity funds are actually based on partnership structures, which also exempt the issuer from a corporate tax. Finally, there is the exchange traded note (ETN), a new entity, which is actually a subordinated debt instrument designed to replicate returns on a particular index. We will return to the topic of ETNs in chapter 7.

THE MARKET FOR ETFs

While some flavors of exchange traded funds have proliferated more than others, as a category, ETFs have grown exponentially in the nearly fifteen years since their launch. As discussed in the introduction, the market continues to grow in terms of both its size and its diversity. Last year, more than 8 percent of trading in American equities was done through an exchange traded fund. While the size of the market, currently more than $400 billion in the United States alone, is still dwarfed by the size of the mutual fund complex at more than $10 trillion, assets in ETFs are growing at a much quicker pace. In 2006, assets in exchange traded funds rose by a bit less than 40 percent, and climbed by an additional $22 billion through March 2007.[10]

While the United States is still the largest market for exchange traded funds, it is not the only market. The global size of the market is now close to $600 billion, with seven hundred different exchange traded funds trading on a total of thirty-eight different exchanges at the end of 2006.

After the United States, Europe is the next largest market. While still small compared to the United States in terms of assets under management, $90 billion versus $406 billion in the United States, the number of ETFs in Europe is starting to catch up. There are 272 different exchange traded funds in Europe versus 343 in the United States. Even though European assets are still small compared to those in the United States, the growth rate is actually quicker in Europe. European listed assets under management increased by 63 percent compared to less than 40 percent in the United States. While some of the increase was a function of stronger markets abroad, European ETFs were gathering assets at a faster rate even after accounting for market movements.[11]

As indicated in the introduction, the market has now become sufficiently deep and diverse to offer investors exposures to most asset classes, countries, sectors, and increasingly specialized markets. The growth in assets has been driven by several factors, including a rising market and increased allocation to existing products. It has also been driven by an ever growing list of new products. In 2006, 279 different ETFs were launched. To put that number in perspective, it is more than twice the 119 funds introduced in 2005, and five times the 52 launched in 2004. Nor is this pace expected to slow down anytime soon. The end of 2007 should see the launch of an additional 516 funds for the year. While the lion's share of that total—423 funds—is expected to occur in the United States, there are also 68 new ETFs scheduled to launch in Europe, with an additional 25 in other countries. It is also worth pointing out that unlike the hedge fund industry where new funds are often simply replacing failed ones, there have been virtually no delistings of ETFs. During all of 2006, only 8 ETFs were removed from exchanges.[12]

While exchange traded funds offer many advantages for the retail investor, their appeal has not been lost on institutional investors. Much of the product's rise and recent popularity can be attributed to large institutions. For sophisticated professional investors, exchange traded funds offer many of the same benefits that they do to retail investors: cheap and efficient beta, a well-diversified list of risk factors, and market liquidity. The last aspect is particularly significant for large institutions that need to be cognizant of the depth of a market in a given security. But for the institutional investor, the list does not stop there. As we touched upon earlier, these funds also offer the possibility of more sophisticated investment strategies, such as shorting, securities lending, and option trading. In addition, they offer a very efficient hedging mechanism.

Let's say a hedge fund likes a particular retail stock, but it believes that overall consumer spending is likely to decline. The investor could purchase the stock, but then hedge the purchase with an offsetting short position in an ETF focused on the retail sector. This trade would effectively "strip" the retail beta from the stock. By doing so, the investor is now betting on the relative performance of the stock versus the rest of the sector. If his or her pick is correct, the stock is likely to outperform the other retailers, producing a profit for the investor, even if the overall sector should decline. This is just one way in which institutional investors can employ exchange traded funds to expand their trading arsenal.

This versatility has made the ETF an increasingly necessary tool for many professional investors. Over the past several years, the number of money managers employing exchange traded funds has continued to grow. Over the course of 2006, there was a 27 percent increase in the number of institutional investors who reported holding either an ETF or HOLDR over the previous year. Over a longer time frame, the growth has been spectacular. Since 2000, the number of institutional users of the product has increased by nearly 350 percent. Not surprisingly, given their increased flexibility over traditional money managers, the number of hedge funds employing ETFs has grown even faster. During 2006, the number of hedge fund managers employing ETFs or HOLDRs grew by more than 60 percent.[13]

While this may represent more competition for the individual investor looking to time a tactical trade in semiconductors, or gain from the next 5 percent move in the Malaysian market, this is not necessarily bad news for the less aggressive individual investor. For those looking to gain broad exposure to different markets, and have an investment rather than a trading focus, the presence of the institutional investor is likely to continue to spur development and innovation. It encourages sponsors to launch new funds with different characteristics. Many of these new funds will provide a broader list of betas, making more markets accessible to ordinary investors. In addition, the presence of large institutional investors helps to ensure liquidity, or "depth" in these markets. This in turn ensures that when you want to buy or sell an ETF, there will be a willing counterparty to take the other side of that trade.

There is a third dimension in which exchange traded funds have also grown. In addition to the increase in the assets under management and the number of funds, there has also been a significant increase in the number of firms that sponsor ETFs. Back in the 1990s the field was limited to a few large players, predominately large index managers such as State Street Global Advisors (SSgA) and Barclays Global Investors (BGI). Over the years, while these two sponsors have continued to build on their offerings, the number of new entrants has mushroomed. In 2006, there were sixteen new ETF sponsors that entered the market. The largest of these is Pro-Funds, with twelve new ETFs and more than $2 billion under management, followed by WisdomTree with assets of more than $1.5 billion in thirty different funds.[14]

While the new entrants into the ETF business have created a more diverse field, the first movers have managed, thus far, to maintain the lion's share of the business. BGI is still the largest manager, with assets of nearly $300 billion, close to a 50 percent market share. The firm has maintained its lead, not only through the continued success of its funds, but also through the creation of new products. In 2006, BGI led the industry in the creation of new exchange traded funds, with a total of 40. This brings the firm's total to 188, the largest in the industry. Boston-based SSgA has also held on to its position at the top of the league tables. State Street remains the second-largest sponsor with more than $100 billion under management and a more than 17 percent market share.[15]

With a market size at over half a trillion dollars, and new versions being added almost daily, the question arises as to how the market got so large so quickly. One of the key reasons that the number of products has been able to grow exponentially is the relative ease with which new funds can be created, and how new money can flow into existing funds. As with an ordinary listed company, or a closed-ended fund, ETFs register their offers and sales under the Securities Act and then list the funds on a securities exchange. Regardless of which structure is employed, the creation of exchange traded funds is the same.

Once the ETF is registered, the creation of new units is a straight-forward concept. In contrast to more traditional open-ended funds,

ETFs issue shares in large blocks (normally in blocks of 50,000 shares) called "creation units." An investor, typically a large institution, may purchase a creation unit with a deposit equal in value to the aggregate NAV of the ETF shares. The manager or sponsor announces the contents of the deposit at the beginning of each trading day. Typically, the institution will deposit a basket of securities that mirrors the portfolio composition of that particular ETF.[16] The amount of stock deposited must be sufficiently large to create at least one creation unit for that particular ETF.

If the institution was looking to create a SPDR, an ETF that tracks the performance of the S&P 500 index, they would deposit the stocks in the index in the amount that matched their weight in the index. A creation unit for the SPDR would require enough stock to create fifty thousand new ETFs based on that particular index (the investor would probably also need to deposit a certain amount of cash in order to cover any accrued dividends). Once the ETF creation unit has been established, the institution can either hold or sell some of the ETFs in the secondary market. This is how the funds go from creation to actively trading on the various exchanges. Again, the presence of large institutional investors in this market helps to provide liquidity and a deep two-way market in these instruments. And while retail investors are likely neither to create nor redeem an ETF unit, it is worth knowing that these instruments can be redeemed in a similar fashion to how they are created. Large institutional investors can exchange their ETFs for the underlying securities. As with the creation of a unit, the redemption must be in a similarly large size. When an investor presents a creation unit for redemption, he or she receives a "redemption basket," which is identified by the ETF sponsor at the beginning of the day. The basket will contain the securities in that index, along with a certain amount of residual cash.[17]

The ability to continually create and redeem units of exchange traded funds is of more than just academic value. In addition to providing liquidity, it also serves another useful purpose. By providing large institutions with a mechanism to arbitrage any mispricings, the cycle of creating and redeeming ETFs keeps their prices roughly in line with those of the underlying basket of securities they hold. Without the ability to redeem ETFs for their underlying shares, and back again, there would be no mechanism for maintaining this balance. Consider the case of the SPDR, which is supposed to trade for one tenth of the value of the S&P 500 Index. If the value of the S&P 500 is 1,500, then the SPDR should theoretically trade close to 150. However, there is no regulatory or legal mechanism that demands that the instrument trade at that level. While 150 represents the value of the underlying securities, or net asset value (NAV), there is nothing preventing investors from temporarily bidding its value higher or lower, depending upon market conditions.

It is not inconceivable that investors could bid up the SPDR above fair value if there was an abrupt need to gain exposure to the market, and the SPDR represented a particularly efficient method for accessing this exposure. Alternatively, there may be an instance, such as a particularly negative news event, when investors would want to take advantage of the liquidity of the SPDR to quickly lower their equity exposure. The rush of investors to sell the same instrument simultaneously could drive the value of the SPDR below the one-tenth ratio described above. Perhaps in this instance, SPDRs would trade for one eleventh of the value of the underlying securities. In other words, the SPDR would be temporarily trading below its NAV.

Even in the above circumstance, what would keep the SPDR fairly close to its fair value is the arbitrage potential that would present itself to a large institution. By arbitrage I'm referring to the ability of traders to simultaneously buy or sell the SPDR and take an offsetting position in the underlying securities. If there was a significant mismatch between the price of the fund and the stocks that make up that fund, a nimble trader could make a riskless profit by buying one and selling the other. If the SPDR declined too abruptly and started to trade at a significant discount to the underlying basket of securities, a large institution could make a profit by purchasing the SPDR in sufficiently large quantities that they could redeem them for the underlying securities. Because the SPDR's value would be less than that of the underlying basket of stocks, a large trader would profit by simply stepping in and acting as the marginal buyer in that market. There are transaction costs associated with the purchase of the SPDR, and the subsequent sale of the underlying security, so the potential profit needs to be large enough to overcome this friction. But for a big institutional investor, who can trade cheaply and is buying millions of dollars of securities, even a small deviation from the NAV may be large enough to justify an arbitrage trade.

The ability to create and redeem shares helps keep the SPDR, as well as other ETFs, close to its underlying NAV. This transaction, or arbitrage, is made more attractive by the fact that the theoretical institution that redeemed their ETFs for the underlying securities would not face a taxable event. Because they are receiving securities, known as an "in-kind distribution," rather than cash, there is no taxable event. In contrast, a more traditional open-ended fund that needed to meet redemptions, and did not have sufficient cash

Types of Funds			
EXAMPLE	LEGAL BASIS	TAX BASIS	CHARACTERISTICS
SPDR, MDY	1940 Act	Grantor trust	Cannot hold securities except as part of unmanaged process. No reinvestment of dividends
iShares	1940 Act, Sub-Chapter M	No corporate tax if full amount distributed to shareholders	Have exemption to 1940 Act requirement for redemption. Only need to redeem to authorized participants in large blocks
HOLDR	Receipt in basket of underlying securities	Grantor trust	No management fee—paid out of dividends. HOLDRs do not rebalance
GLD, Ryder Currency funds	Grantor trust	Grantor trust	Underlying holding not securities
USO	Publicly traded partnership	No corporate tax as partnership	Mostly used in commodity funds

on hand, would need to sell securities to raise the cash.[18] This sale of the securities would represent a taxable event to the underlying investors.

There are additional real-world frictions that will cause an ETF to deviate from its NAV, despite the best interest of large arbitrageurs. Most of this drift is a function of the way that cash is accounted for in the funds. Earlier in the chapter, I illustrated how different types of funds have distinct policies for dealing with dividends. In the case of the exchange traded fund, the value of the fund should equal the underlying value of the securities plus any undistributed net income. The undistributed net income is composed of two distinct parts: estimated cash per unit and a second portion known as the distribution price adjustment. The cash amount is the total of dividends received by the fund but not yet distributed.[19] This is because the exchange traded fund does not immediately pass out the dividends to the holders of the fund, but rather accrues them and then pays them out on a regularly scheduled basis, normally quarterly. The second component of the undistributed net income, the distribution price adjustment, reflects an amount per unit that has been declared as a distribution, but not yet paid to the unit holders. Usually the distribution adjustment will be zero, since there are usually only a few days in the quarter between the declaration of distributions and their payout to fund holders.[20]

For most individual investors, the precise details of the manner in which NAV is calculated or dividends are accrued will have little impact on their investment decisions. Probably the most important consideration is to ensure that the fund you're buying is not trading at an amount significantly above the value of the underlying securities and the accrued dividends. If you are paying a premium, you are in effect paying more for the basket of securities than you would if you purchased them individually. If the premium is very small, this may not be a significant concern, as there would be additional transaction costs if you attempted to purchase all the stocks in a given index. In addition, your portfolio may not be of adequate size to purchase all of the securities in an index, hence the value of the ETF in the first place. However, there may be instances where the premium has pushed the ETF's price significantly above the NAV. In such cases, it may make sense to see if there is another ETF that offers a similar exposure. For example, several sponsors offer exchange traded funds tied to technology indices. One of the criteria an investor should use when deciding between them is the relationship between the ETF's current price and the NAV. It may be that a similar product can gain you the same exposure, without having to pay any premium (think of premiums as another manifestation of transaction costs, something you want to minimize).

COSTS OF TRADING

Comparing an ETF's price to its underlying NAV is a useful exercise, but there are other considerations in deciding which instrument to purchase. While there is no point in paying a premium for an ETF, there are other costs to consider as well, including the costs of trading and the management fees associated with the fund. The latter is likely to be the single biggest cost associated with owning an ETF. As mentioned above, unlike traditional mutual funds, there is no subscription or redemption fee. When you buy or sell an exchange traded fund, your only cost is the commission you pay to your broker. In contrast, many mutual funds will assess a sales charge, which can either be paid up front, or upon redemption, known as a back-end-loaded fund. However, ETFs do charge management fees, and these can vary considerably from product to product (I will highlight many of the management fees for popular funds in the following chapters). A general rule is: the more exotic the beta, the higher the fee. An ETF based on a popular domestic index, such as the S&P 500, should charge only a small management fee, perhaps somewhere between 0.10 percent and 0.30 percent per year. More specific indices, such as sector funds, are likely to charge a bit more.

The largest fees are likely to be found for funds tracking an international index, particularly emerging markets. However, even in those instances where the management fee is relatively high compared to other exchange traded funds, it is likely to be considerably cheaper than the average active mutual fund. Since ETFs do not require a portfolio manager or research team to select securities or build a portfolio, they are much cheaper for the sponsors to run, and therefore incur much lower fees. The average ETF has a 0.41 percent expense ratio. This is less than one third of the 1.35 percent average for actively managed mutual funds.[21]

Now, as exchange traded funds are not actively managed, this is a bit of an unfair comparison. A better comparison is how ETFs compare to index funds, which also replicate the exposure of a particular index without trying to outperform it. Even when compared to more traditional index funds, ETFs still appear cheap. Their average management fee of 0.41 percent is almost half of the average index fund's, at 0.74 percent.[22] Obviously, the averages mask some variation in the fees, which can vary significantly from fund to fund. For index ETFs that are registered investment companies, annual management fees range from 0.09 percent to 0.99 percent of the fund assets. However, this does not tell the whole story, as both traditional mutual funds, as well as exchange traded funds, have some smaller fees that can affect the relative costs. For example, certain ETFs, which are not registered as investment companies, also register a 0.08 percent custody fee if any of the underlying stocks pays a dividend.[23] On the traditional fund side, many mutual funds charge what is known as a 12b-1 fee. This is a fee mutual funds may charge that allows them to recoup costs associated with the distribution of the fund's shares. In contrast, ETFs do not charge any 12b-1 fees.

So, while exchange traded funds generally have lower management fees than traditional index funds, and much lower management fees than active funds, there are other costs involved for each type of investment vehicle. These other costs may, depending upon the circumstances of the individual investor, change the overall advantage of one product versus another. In determining the cheaper solution, it is worth considering the size of your portfolio, your frequency of trading, and your trading costs (remember, unlike traditional mutual funds, ETFs must be purchased like a stock, so the price at which you can execute will be one determinant of your overall cost structure). For small investors, index funds do offer one significant advantage over exchange traded funds. They generally incur no load, nor do they require paying a broker a commission. In effect, you can purchase an index fund ostensibly for free. In contrast, an ETF is purchased like a stock, and in doing so, you will incur commission costs when you buy and sell the fund.

Purchasing an ETF in the market will entail several costs, including commissions and the bid-ask spread. (A bid-ask spread is the difference between what it costs you to buy a security versus what you could sell it at. This difference is another hidden cost that benefits your broker.) For this discussion, I will ignore market impact as a trading cost, as the typical trade of even a large retail investor is unlikely to have a significant impact on the price of the fund. The first cost to note is brokerage commission, which will vary from individual to individual depending upon their fee structure with a brokerage firm. Assuming our hypothetical small investor has an account with a typical discount broker, they are probably going to pay a commission of approximately $9 per trade, or $18 "round trip." In other words, it will cost them $18 to buy and then eventually sell the fund.

In addition to the commission, there may be a bid-ask spread. For ETFs based on larger indices, this is probably a negligible cost of a few pennies, but it may be more significant for smaller, less liquid ETFs. It is not unreasonable that for a smaller industry or sector fund, the spread could be on the order of 0.25 percent of the trade's cost. Assuming a small, hypothetical $200 allocation to an ETF, the combined costs between the spread and the commission would be $18.50. While this might constitute a reasonable transaction cost for a purchase of several thousand dollars, it is prohibitively expensive for a trade of $200, where the commission plus spread is now equal to nearly 10 percent of the investment. In this instance, an ETF might not be the right investment vehicle for a small investor starting out, or one using dollar cost averaging. Generally, the cost savings for ETFs will be more apparent for an investor who already has a reasonably sized portfolio.[24] So for an investor with a small portfolio, or one who makes frequent small incremental investments, an index fund may be the more economical vehicle.

No discussion of the costs of an investment product would be complete without a discussion of the tax implications. As discussed above, one of the primary motivations for different fund structures has been the need to create entities that are exempt from corporate taxation. While the funds themselves do not pay taxes, there are still significant tax implications for those who invest in exchange traded funds. For that reason, investors should have a solid grasp of the tax implications of the funds. Given the persistent complexities of the current tax code, instruments that appear cheap can take on a very different character when tax considerations are factored in. Likewise, some instruments that make little sense on their own appear considerably more attractive when the nuances of the tax code are taken into account. As with any investment, individuals should confirm their own tax status with a tax professional, but for the most part, exchange traded funds are fairly straightforward when it comes to their tax implications.

Except in instances described below, exchange traded funds will generate a tax event upon their disposition or the paying of dividends. As with other instruments, and subject to the extension of the 2003 tax cuts, capital gains and dividends are taxed at preferential rates when compared to ordinary income. What makes exchange traded funds attractive from a tax standpoint is that they minimize the amount of taxable gains not derived from the disposition of the fund. In other words, ETFs provide greater control on the timing of when taxable events occur. The difference is that you pay a tax only when you decide to sell, rather than when the fund manager decides to sell.

Experts generally agree that exchange traded funds are a more tax-efficient product than traditional open-ended mutual funds. The advantage of ETFs lies in the previous discussion of how they handle redemptions, versus the mechanism used by a typical mutual fund. Mutual funds are penalized if they keep excess cash on hand. All mutual funds are measured against some type of benchmark, such as the Russell 2000. The larger their cash position, the less they have invested in stocks, and the harder it is to beat that benchmark. The reason is that in contrast to any real-life fund, all the money in the theoretical benchmark is invested in the market. Therefore, portfolio managers generally keep a very small portion of their portfolio in cash, usually less than 7 to 8 percent, and often as little as 3 or 4 percent. As the fund does not hold much cash, the fund manager is often forced to sell securities in order to generate the cash needed to meet redemptions. In those instances, if the securities they are selling have appreciated in price, a capital gains tax is assessed and passed on to the holders or investors of the fund. It is possible that even if the fund is down for the year, it could generate capital gains if the fund manager was forced to sell some of the stocks that had risen that year (a real possibility as those names may provide the best liquidity in the event of a severe market correction). The need to sell securities to generate cash can be very tax inefficient under certain circumstances. There are few investment scenarios more frustrating than having your mutual fund go down for the year, and getting a tax bill on top of it.

Because of the difference in how exchange traded funds are created and redeemed, they are normally immune to the type of problem described above. If an investor wants to sell a fund, there is a liquid market available to absorb that trade. The fund does not need to sell securities in order to provide the investor with his or her cash back. So it is rare, although not impossible, for an ETF to generate a capital gain without a sale of the instrument. One set of conditions that could generate a taxable event without a sale of the fund would be if a company held by the ETF was acquired for a premium, or if the composition of the underlying index changed. However, for the most part, several factors conspire to make ETFs less susceptible to distributed capital gains than ordinary funds. First, until now exchange traded funds have all been index funds, and thus have much lower turnover than traditional active funds. Second, as investors trade actual ETF shares with each other rather than buying or redeeming directly from the fund manager (except in the case of large institutions), the managers do not have to sell securities to pay off redemptions. Finally, in those instances when large institutions do redeem, it is an in-kind redemption, and therefore does not trigger a taxable event. Given these differences from traditional mutual funds, exchange traded funds do indeed appear to offer a more tax-efficient vehicle.

Looking at the tax-cost ratios (which measure how much a fund's annualized return is reduced by the taxes that an investor in the highest tax bracket would pay on distributions) demonstrates the tax efficiency of ETFs versus traditional funds. A recent study examined the tax-cost ratios for ETFs that have been around at least five years. In six of the nine diversified domestic stock fund categories, the average ETF had a lower five-year tax-cost ratio through the end of January 2006 than a typical open-end mutual fund.[25] While exchange traded funds tend to generate lower capital gains than equivalent traditional funds, there are exceptions to this rule. In general, ETFs showed a consistent advantage in mid-cap and small-cap funds along with growth funds. What these strategies have in common is high turnover, which can generate high capital gains in traditional fund structures. However, in the large-cap arena, traditional funds maintained an advantage when it came to tax-cost ratios. While ETFs trailed in this category, for the vast majority of categories, including international funds, ETFs with five-year track records ranked in the lowest half of their fund categories.[26] Those exchange traded funds that fell in the top half of their respective categories were generally those with high turnover (i.e., a high degree of trading). One explanation for what was generating that high turnover may have been a change in the benchmark index on which the ETF is based. A change in the underlying benchmark would require that the ETF change its weighting, and potentially the securities, in its portfolio.

Distributed capital gains are not the only way to affect the tax consequences of holding an ETF. Income may be equally important and,

---

Benefits and Uses of ETFs for Individual Versus Institutional Investors

INDIVIDUAL

- Low cost, cheap beta
- Easy to buy and sell
- Tax efficient

INSTITUTIONAL

- Liquid instruments; can trade in size
- Flexibility; can use them to establish "inverse" positions or leveraged bets
- Often cheaper and more efficient than trading a basket of stocks

---

in the case of certain high-yielding equity indices such as utilities or real estate investment trusts (REITs), may have more significance for the overall tax bill. For example, investments in REIT ETFs can create higher tax liabilities as neither REIT income nor return of capital qualifies for the lower 15 percent tax rate. Instead, it is taxed as ordinary income. Of course, an investor would face the same tax implications if he or she held the REIT directly. In general, ETFs are fairly tax efficient. There are relatively few instances where the particular characteristics of a fund are likely to result in a higher tax bill than a similar holding in a traditional mutual fund or the underlying stocks.

ETFs AND BETA: GETTING WHAT YOU PAID FOR

As with any purchase, comparing the costs of competing products is a prudent exercise. In addition to costs, investors also need to ask another basic question: are they getting what they paid for? In the case of an exchange traded fund, the measure of that question is whether the fund provides the requisite exposure to the given index or market. When you select a particular exchange traded fund, you are expecting exposure, or beta, to a certain type of asset. We previously discussed how the construction of HOLDRs could theoretically lead to a deviation from the beta exposure for which the instrument was originally intended. HOLDRs are not alone in that respect. There are other ways in which different fund structures can also diverge from their benchmarks. This is an important consideration in selecting an ETF, as a significant deviation from the original benchmark may leave you with an exposure you did not intend, or fail to provide you with the original beta you were looking for.

This issue has appeared in a number of new funds, and tends to be more prevalent in those ETFs that seek to track narrower, more esoteric indices. This has been most evident in some of the new commodity-focused ETFs. One recent example was Victoria Bay Asset Management's U.S. Oil Fund. This fund's returns have recently fallen significantly behind the price of crude oil, which it purports to track. A similar problem happened to an ETF from Claymore Securities, only in this case the price of the fund actually fell while crude oil prices rose. While the exact causes of the discrepancy are not entirely clear, they are tied to the cost of rolling over futures contracts each month.[27] As these funds are based on a single commodity, it is somewhat easier for performance to deviate. This is because of the complexities of managing the underlying futures positions as they move, or "roll," from one month to the next. With narrower funds that rely on fewer instruments there is more potential for this type of a divergence.

Creating an ETF and Dissolving an ETF

STEP 1.

Large institutional investor, an authorized participant (AP), transfers a portfolio of stocks to a fund manager. The portfolio will mimic an index, such as the S&P 500.

STEP 2.

The fund manager receives the stock into a legal entity such as a trust, and issues ETF shares to the AP, who can then sell the ETF shares to other investors. This technique is referred to as "in-kind," because the ETF shares are issued for a basket of stocks rather than cash.

STEP 3.

Once issued, the ETF shares can trade on an exchange like any other security.

STEP 4.

When a large institutional holder wants to retire its ETF shares, that investor can trade it back and receive the stocks that make up the ETF.

The critical test of an exchange traded fund is to ensure that its performance closely tracks the index it represents. The inclusion of a particular ETF in a portfolio indicates a desire for the beta of the underlying index. If an exchange traded fund produces a return that differs from that index, you are not getting a good approximation of that beta. Small deviations should not be a source of concern, as short-term trading idiosyncrasies may cause a fund's performance to deviate from the benchmark for a brief period of time. However, if over a longer time frame—months or a few quarters—the performance of an ETF is materially different from that of the index, then the fund is not doing its job. One of the key benefits to an ETF is its simplicity. It tracks an index, rather than trying to outperform it.

This is the main reason ETFs are cheaper than traditional funds. Evaluating an index fund, whether an ETF or a traditional index fund, is a matter of measuring the "tracking error," or the extent to which the fund deviates from its benchmark. The lower the tracking error, the closer the ETF is to approximating its specific benchmark. Tracking error, along with price, should be one of the primary determinants of which ETF to purchase. Having laid out the case, costs, and concerns of the product, we will now turn to the larger question of how to combine these instruments into a robust and cost-efficient portfolio.

Chapter 5

EQUITY ETFS: SECTORS, COUNTRIES, AND STYLES

O nce you understand the concept of risk exposures, the next challenge is to utilize ETFs to gain access to those different betas. The rest of this book will focus on using exchange traded funds to leverage your portfolio to different types of betas. To that end, the next several chapters will be organized around different asset classes: equities, fixed income, and commodities. Most investors will be the most experienced with equities as an investment vehicle. Not coincidentally, this is also the asset class where exchange traded funds were first introduced and where longevity has created the deepest and most diverse market. There are not only more equity ETFs than any other asset class, there is also more diversity and liquidity in these instruments.

While asset allocation is not the focus of this book, a few words on it will help frame the conversation. Financial advisers generally assume a mix of assets in an individual portfolio, with the mix tilted toward equities during a person's working years, and shifting toward fixed income, or income-producing securities, as individuals near retirement. The exact amounts of the mix are a function of age, financial needs, and the risk tolerance of the investors. Generally, the more risk tolerant the investor, the higher the allocation to equities. In addition, for most working-age investors, equities are and should be the largest portion of their portfolio.

Over the long term, defined as twenty or more years, stocks have consistently outperformed all other asset classes, and have also offered a better hedge against inflation than fixed-income securities. Most financial planners generally recommend an equity allocation somewhere in the 50 percent to 70 percent range for individuals under fifty. With life expectancies rising, some planners are advising their clients to have a majority of their portfolio in stocks, even after the age of fifty. As people live longer, the long-term potential erosion of income to inflation becomes a significant concern. For this reason, even older individuals want to maintain a significant weighting to equity securities to protect the purchasing power of their assets.

Beyond equities and fixed-income securities, an increasing number of financial advisers will also advocate holding a small position in other asset classes, such as commodities. One of the main advantages of these different asset classes is that they have historically had a low correlation with equities. In addition to their low correlation with other asset classes, commodities also act as a natural hedge against inflation and erosion of purchasing power. Beyond commodities, there are other forms of asset classes, such as real estate. For wealthier individuals, the allocation can also include a percentage of alternative asset classes such as hedge funds or private equity. While not every investment or asset class can be replicated with exchange traded funds, the number is growing rapidly.

For the purposes of the remainder of this book, I will assume that investors are looking to gain exposure to multiple asset classes, and are seeking to gain that exposure through exchange traded funds. Included in the discussion will be some more exotic asset classes such as real estate or private equity. The purpose of including these more esoteric assets in the discussion is not to advocate major allocations to them, but merely to illustrate the diversifying benefits of small allocations to nontraditional assets, and to demonstrate ways to gain that exposure through ETFs. The exact amount that should be allocated to these types of products is, again, a function of age, means, and risk tolerance.

For the purpose of this discussion, I will largely ignore the question of how much to allocate between the different classes, as that is well outside the scope of this book, and a better topic for a conversation with a financial adviser. As equities compose the largest section of most people's portfolio, I will start the conversation there. Equities also provide a useful starting point with which to begin thinking about portfolios in a different light. As discussed in chapter 4, when most individual investors consider their equity holdings, they think in terms of the stocks they own. This is quite natural, but potentially a limiting way to build a portfolio. Each stock in your portfolio also represents exposures to different risks. Together, those risks aggregate up to the portfolio level. The critical question to ask is, what risk exposures do you want in the equity portion of your portfolio, and how can you arrive at those exposures? For the purposes of this analysis, we will focus on three separate dimensions of exposures: sector or industry, style, and country or region. The first exposure refers to the economic sector of a particular stock—the stock's principal line of business. The second, style, measures either the size of the company or whether it is a growth or a value stock. The final category relates a company to its home country, or where it is domiciled.

SECTOR INVESTING: ORGANIZING THE MARKET

Starting with sector or industry exposure, this type of risk exposure pertains to the business and economic sensitivity of the companies. Firms are grouped into categories based on their primary business, with these businesses sharing certain characteristics. Most classification schemes generally segment stocks into one of ten economic sectors:

- energy
- materials
- industrials
- consumer discretionary
- consumer staples
- financials
- health care
- technology
- telecom
- utilities

Most of these sectors are self-explanatory, and simply refer to the business of a company. Two of the sectors that merit additional clarification are consumer discretionary and consumer staples. Consumer discretionary refers to companies catering to consumer spending that is more economically sensitive. Stocks in this industry include retailers, restaurants, hotels, and apparel. In contrast, stocks in the consumer staples sector are those in industries that are less affected by the overall economy. These are companies that produce products consumers purchase in good times and bad. Companies involved in cosmetics, food and beverages, and home products would be in this category. These products are considered more basic, and have more stable sales cycles, while consumer discretionary stocks tend to be more cyclical in nature.

Sectors can be further cut into more granular components, generally referred to as industries or groups. For example, within technology there are several separate industries, such as semiconductors, software, hardware, and communication equipment. Industry or group classifications provide for more granular categories, with the companies in a given industry having even more in common than those within a sector. While industries within a sector generally share similar characteristics in terms of their cyclicality and economic dependencies, there are differences.

Take the example of the industrials sector. There are several industries within this sector, including machinery and aerospace and defense. While both are dependent upon capital spending, nuances of their business models actually make these industries very distinct. Much of the machinery industry is dominated by two stocks: Caterpillar and Deere. The first stock's fortunes are largely tied to construction activity, while Deere is linked to the demand for farm equipment.

In contrast, many of the stocks in aerospace and defense are leveraged to government defense spending. Not only is this industry less cyclical, but it is also tied to government rather than private consumption. As defense spending has steadily risen over the past six years, the revenue of these companies has followed a different cycle from other industrial industries. While both machinery and aerospace and defense are in the same sector and depend on capital spending, both their customer bases and cycles differ dramatically. ETFs based on an industry are more targeted and leveraged to more specific risk factors than those based on a sector definition. Changes in defense spending are likely to have a less dramatic impact on an ETF indexed to the industrial sector than on one that focuses exclusively on aerospace and defense firms.

There are exchange traded funds available for sectors and industries, with additional exchange traded funds available for international and global sectors as well. So, for example, within financials State Street Global Advisors offers the Financial Select Sector SPDR Fund (XLF), which is intended to provide coverage for the entire sector. To that extent, the product has a mix of exposures between large banks (Citigroup and Bank of America), insurance (AIG), capital markets (Goldman Sachs and Morgan Stanley), and consumer finance (American Express). The XLF will provide broad exposure to the entire U.S. financial sector. However, there are other funds that provide a more targeted risk exposure.

Other popular ETFs may focus on just one of the industries within financials, such as commercial banks, insurance, diversified financials, or REITs. For investors who want to focus on the REITs industry, a very specific subset of financials, there is the iShares Cohen & Steers Realty Majors Index Fund (ICF), which tracks an index of large REITs. There is another iShares available from BGI that focuses exclusively on U.S. broker dealers, the iShares Dow Jones U.S. Broker-Dealer Index Fund (IAI). And if an investor wants to concentrate his or her financial exposure within the banking industry, there is the Regional Bank HOLDR (RKH). While all of these instruments are considered financials, they have some distinct characteristics. Banks are likely to be more interest rate sensitive than brokers. If you are looking to leverage to the recent surge in M&A activity, the REIT ETF is unlikely to provide much exposure, and you would be better off with the IAI. Likewise, the REIT ETF will provide not only better leverage to the real estate market, but also a higher dividend yield (with different tax implications as highlighted in the previous chapter). So when selecting between sector and industry funds, an investor needs to be aware of the breadth of exposure he or she is getting. Generally speaking, the sector-oriented funds provide better diversification than the industry funds, which are based on narrower, more idiosyncratic indices.

Price should be another consideration when choosing between sector and industry funds. Consistent with the rule that more exotic or specific beta costs more, sector funds are generally cheaper than industry funds. State Street and Vanguard's sector funds charge approximately 0.25 percent in annual fees. In contrast, industry exchange traded funds tend to be a bit more expensive. On the low end, industry-oriented ETFs sponsored by State Street trade with a 0.35 percent expense fee. Most sponsors charge a bit more. The iShare industry funds incur an expense ratio of a bit less than 0.50 percent, with prices rising as high as 0.70 percent for some of the smaller providers. Again, if an investor has a precise insight justifying a position in an industry fund, the additional cost may be worth it. In the absence of any information, investors looking to incorporate industry or sector exposure should realize that the more precise beta comes with a modestly higher price tag.

There is another nuance to sector investing that investors should consider. Most exchange traded funds, as with most indices, are weighted by the market capitalization, or market cap, of the stocks in that index. In this sense, the larger companies, measured by their market value, have the largest weighting. (The exception to this rule is the Dow Industrials, for which funds are price weighted—the higher the price of the stock the larger its weight in the index.) Market cap-weighted indices have disproportionately large weights to the bigger companies. For example, within the GICS Application Software Sub-Industry Index, Microsoft (MSFT) accounts for upward of 40 percent of the index. In some industries, two or three large names can dominate the index. In order to address this, there is a group of funds sponsored by Rydex Investments that offer sector exposure based on an equally weighted index (they also offer an S&P 500 exchange traded fund based on an equally weighted index). These funds are based on the S&P Equal Weight indices for nine of the ten GICS (Global Industry Classification Standard) sectors (telecom is excluded). The benefit of these products is that the index on which the fund is based is broader, and less influenced by a particular stock or stocks. However, there will be some differential in returns between these products and the more frequently quoted cap-weighted indices. For example, an investor who purchased the Rydex S&P Equal Weight ETF (RSP) would do better than the SPDR in an environment in which the smaller stocks in the index were stronger than the largest, "megacap" stocks. However, in an environment where a few large stocks produced the majority of the gains, you would be likely to underperform.

When looking to choose between an equal-weighted and cap-weighted ETF, investors should not ignore the fees. For example, consider the cap-weighted SPDR as compared with the RSP. The former charges a management fee of just 0.11 percent, versus 0.40 percent for the RSP.[1] The higher fee is a function of the fact that the equal-weighted S&P 500 index is slightly more exotic, and therefore tends to command a higher fee. In order to justify the higher fee, an investor would need to believe either that an equally weighted index provides lower risk because of less concentrated stock-specific risk, or that the smaller names in the index will outperform in the long run, thereby producing a relatively higher return for the equal-weighted product. Since 1975, the annualized return on the equal weighted has outperformed the cap weighted by approximately 0.15 percent per year, even after taking the fees into account. The outperformance of the RSP is largely a function of the strength in midcap names since 2000.[2]

Before concluding that investing in equal-weighted indices is the answer, investors should consider two additional facts that make the case for any one construction more ambiguous. First, the nominally higher return in the equal-weighted index was accompanied by higher risk. The equal-weighted index had an annual standard deviation of returns of 17.68 percent versus 15.14 percent for the cap weighted. This is a significant difference, and on a risk-adjusted basis more than cancels out the benefit of 0.15 percent in incremental returns. In addition, when you look at the composition of the two indices you also find that the market-cap variation has more of a value tilt to it, with lower price-to-earnings and price-to-cash flow as well as a higher dividend yield.[3] So the characteristics of the two products, while both based on the same constituent universe, are very different given their different weighting schemes. Investors choosing between the two should ask the same questions as they would when choosing between any other investment products. What are the fees, risk-adjusted returns, and risk characteristics of the various products?

Finally, when considering sector exposure, an investor should also consider the geographic breadth of the sectors. Many funds have expanded their sector exposure outside of the United States. For example, rather than focusing only on companies located in the United States, the iShares S&P Global Financials Sector Index Fund (IXG) includes many international companies within the financials sector, including HSBC Holdings, UBS AG, Banco Santander, and Mitsubishi UFJ Financial. So the sector-risk exposures can vary depending upon both the granularity of the index (sector versus industry) and the physical location (domestic, non-U.S., or global). The issue of geography will be more of a consideration for some industries than for others. Certain sectors, notably materials, energy, and parts of technology, tend to be dominated by global trends and commodity pricing. As a result, the securities in these industries tend to be highly correlated, regardless of where the company is actually domiciled (high oil prices benefit all energy companies). In these instances, the performance of an ETF with a global or domestic mandate is likely to be similar, as the underlying stocks are more likely to trade in line with one another. However, other industries such as consumer discretionary or financials are likely to be highly influenced by local conditions, such as interest rates or the state of the domestic economy. In these instances, the diversification benefit of global coverage can lead to very different returns when compared to a domestically focused ETF in the same industry.

It is also possible that valuation considerations may lead an investor to favor either a domestic, regional, or global ETF. If an investor believed that energy prices were likely to rise, but that valuations for U.S. energy companies already reflected this contingency, perhaps energy companies in other parts of the world are trading at a relative discount. Under that scenario, and assuming other factors are equal, a sector ETF with international exposure may be a more effective way to play the theme of a bull market in energy.

STYLE INVESTING: SIZE AND VALUE

A second dimension of equity risk exposures is investment styles. Equity styles can encompass a broad list of risk factors, but for the purposes of investing in exchange traded funds, we will focus on the two most popular: size, and value versus growth. The first is self-explanatory, and simply refers to the size or market capitalization of a company. Investors generally place companies in different buckets depending upon the market value of the firm, with market value roughly defined as the number of shares outstanding times the current price of the stock. Most investors think in terms of three categories, or buckets: large-cap, midcap, and small-cap (some investors do go further and talk about megacap or microcap stocks as well). While the definition of what constitutes a large- or midcap can differ, large-caps are generally taken to be stocks with a value above the $10 billion range. The midcap bucket is viewed as somewhere between $2 billion and $10 billion, with small-caps anything under that level.

Style, defined by market cap, is a particularly easy category to gain exposure to with an ETF. Many of the most liquid funds are dedicated to style investing. In the U.S. large-cap arena there are several, including:

- SPDR (SPY)
- iShares S&P 500 Index Fund (IVV)

- iShares Russell 1000 Index Fund (IWB)
- iShares S&P 100 Index Fund (OEF)
- DIAMONDS Trust (DIA)

While all are large, liquid funds, the primary difference is in the breadth of their holdings, which is mostly denoted in the names. The DIAMONDS is the narrowest of the indices, with just thirty names, while the Russell 1000 is the broadest, encompassing the one thousand largest names by market cap. While the indices should closely track one another, be aware that particularly narrow indices are the most likely to diverge. In this case, the DIAMONDS is likely to be the most idiosyncratic of the five given its relatively small universe.

The DIAMONDS tracks the Dow Jones Industrial Average, and trades at approximately one one-hundredth of its value. While this index is often the best known to many investors given its longevity and pedigree, it is also the most arbitrary in terms of its construction and the members. Given the relatively small number of companies in the index, and its unusual weighting scheme (a stock's weight in the index is a function of its price, rather than its market cap), the performance of the DIAMONDS can diverge from other large-cap indices. If an investor is specifically looking for exposure to the Dow Industrials, then this is the best instrument. However, if the goal is to obtain more generic, large-cap exposure, the SPY, IVV, or IWB are likely to provide a better match. As all of these funds trade with a very low expense ratio, 0.20 percent or less, gaining the right beta is probably a larger consideration than the relatively small discrepancies in the cost.

In the midcap space, the largest and most popular fund is the SPDR MidCap 400 (MDY), which tracks the S&P MidCap 400

Index. The main competitor to the MDY is the iShares Russell Mid-cap Index Fund (IWR). This fund is based on the Russell set of indices rather than the Standard & Poor's. The IWR tracks midcap stocks—defined as the smallest eight hundred companies within the Russell 1000 Index. The MDY is the larger of the two funds with approximately $9.5 billion in assets, versus a bit under $4 billion for the IWR. The expense ratio is slightly lower for the IWR as opposed to the MDY, at 0.20 percent and 0.25 percent respectively. Unlike the case with the DIAMONDS versus the SPDR, both these funds should provide similar exposure to U.S. midcap names. Since the fall of 2001, the correlation between the two strategies has been more than 96 percent, based on weekly returns.

Finishing up the market-cap spectrum, there are at least two very liquid vehicles to choose from in small-cap. The two most popular small-cap indices are the Russell 2000 and the S&P 600, both of which are represented by an ETF. The larger of the two, measured by net asset value, is the iShares Russell 2000 Index Fund (IWM). This is one of the largest ETFs, with more than $8 billion under management. The ETF representing the S&P 600 index is also an iShares product. The iShares S&P SmallCap 600 Index Fund (IJR) has roughly $4.5 billion in assets. As with the midcap space, these two funds have very similar performance characteristics, as well as similar fees. Both funds charge a 0.20 percent management fee, in line with the fees on the midcap products.

As mentioned previously, the second common dimension in investment styles is value versus growth. While investors may differ about the exact dividing line between large- and midcap, or what constitutes a small-cap versus a microcap, at least they generally agree on how to measure market cap. The value growth divide is a bit murkier, as there are several competing definitions of what constitutes value or growth as an investment style. Some benchmarks base their definition on one metric, such as a price-to-book ratio, with the more expensive stocks in a given universe defined as growth while the cheaper ones are defined as value. Other schemes are more complicated and rely on multiple metrics, including valuation as well as past and expected earnings growth rates. Because growth and value are more difficult to define than market cap, investors are more likely to witness significant departures in performance in this dimension of style versus market cap.

There are a number of both growth and value exchange traded funds across the market-cap spectrum. In U.S. large-cap, BGI offers two large-cap growth ETFs, one based on the Russell classification and one based on the S&P 500. The iShares Russell 1000 Growth Index Fund (IWF) is the larger of the two, with more than $6 billion in assets. The second fund is the iShares S&P 500 Growth Index Fund (IVW), with slightly less than $4 billion under management. However, the S&P 500 Growth fund is the slightly cheaper one, with an expense ratio of 0.18 percent versus 0.20 percent for the IWF. In this instance, the difference in methodology has not had a discernible impact on performance. Both funds have tended to move together, and since 2001 have shared a correlation of nearly 97 percent based on weekly returns.

Similar to the large-cap arena, there are two U.S. midcap growth ETFs, the iShares S&P MidCap Growth Index Fund (IJK) and the iShares Russell MidCap Growth Index Fund (IWP). Both funds are similar in size, with approximately $2 billion in assets, and fees, at 0.25 percent (you can see that as the funds get more specific and farther down in the market capitalization scale, fees start to rise). Finally, there are also two iShares small-cap products, including both a Russell and S&P benchmarked growth index: the iShares Russell 2000 Growth Index Fund (IWO) and the iShares S&P Small-Cap 600 Growth Index Fund (IJT). IWO is the larger of the two, with more than twice the assets, more than $3 billion to less than $1.5 billion for the IJT. In terms of fees, the two are identical, with both charging a 0.25 percent management fee.

For each of the growth-oriented ETFs described above, there is a corresponding value ETF as well. Interestingly, the value ETFs tend to be slightly larger and more liquid than their growth counterparts. This may be a reflection of the fact that value has outperformed growth in most periods since the technology bubble burst in 2000. As with the growth ETFs, pricing between the Russell-benchmarked and the S&P-benchmarked indices does not differ significantly, and tends to be in the 0.20 percent to 0.25 percent range. In the large-cap value ETF space the two major entrants are the iShares Russell 1000 Value Index Fund (IWD) and the iShares S&P 500 Value Index Fund (IVE). The iShares Russell MidCap Value Index Fund (IWS) is the larger of the two midcap products, with approximately $4 billion under management. The slightly smaller iShares S&P 400 MidCap Value Index Fund (IJJ) has just under $3 billion. Finally, the iShares Russell 2000 Value Fund (IWN) is a particularly popular ETF thanks to the recent outperformance of small-cap value in the United States. The fund has more than $4.6 billion under management and trades an average of more than 1.5 million shares per day. Rounding out the small-cap value list is the iShares S&P SmallCap Value Index Fund with a market capitalization of slightly more than $2 billion.

In most of the discussion so far, I've refrained from recommending one sector or another, and I'll continue to dodge that bullet in subsequent chapters. The reason is that investors should strive for a balance in their portfolio, and in the absence of information try to avoid sector timing, as there is little evidence that individuals have been able to add value in this aspect any more than they have in stock selection. However, in the arena of style selection, investors may want to consider adopting a long-term value bias. The argument for this position is that there is a good deal of empirical evidence that over the long term, value investing has produced higher returns. This is not to suggest that value will outperform in any and all periods, as the late 1990s painfully demonstrated. Rather, for long-term investors who are able to ride out cyclical preferences, investing in securities with low price-to-earnings and similar measures produces superior returns. With the proliferation of the various style funds described above, this is now an investment theme individuals can leverage in a cheap and efficient manner.

The academic evidence for value outperformance has been well documented. A recent study by Frank Russell Co. and Bernstein demonstrated that in the period between 1979 and 2003 the Russell 1000 Value Index returned 14.5 percent versus 12.5 percent for the Growth Index.[4] Other studies confirm that this is not merely a U.S. large-cap phenomenon. The same pattern held for small-cap stocks. During the same period, the Russell 2000 Value beat the Russell 2000 Growth, with returns of 15.65 percent and 10.21 percent respectively. Value outperformance also holds outside of the United States. Looking at the MSCI EAFE indices as a proxy for non-U.S. stocks, we find the same outperformance by value. Based on annual returns, the EAFE value index outperformed the EAFE growth components in twenty of twenty-seven years, or 74 percent of the time. In terms of magnitude, the value stocks averaged a

4.2 percent performance premium when compared to their growth counterparts. Using a slightly different methodology, on a rolling five-year basis, value outperformed in twenty-two of the twenty-three five-year periods.[5]

As investors have been conditioned to hearing, past performance is no guarantee of future results. No universal law compels value outperformance, but the long-term track record is impressive, and is also supported by the intuitive notion that paying less for something, including financial assets, is generally a good thing. While academics have been at pains to explain why this seemingly obvious market inefficiency has persisted for as long as it has, the evidence exists and is worth remembering by all investors. Indeed, a good portion of the quants described in chapter 2 spend considerable time and effort in an attempt to define and discover new value opportunities.

Those investors who do choose to overweight value relative to growth should be aware of how this may affect other aspects of their portfolio, particularly their sector positions. Sector composition differs considerably between growth and value stocks. Financials tend to dominate the value universe, while health care, consumer staples, and technology predominate in growth. An investor who leveraged much of their portfolio exposure to value might find that they are underweight in health care and technology compared to the broader indices. This can be rectified by investing directly in these sectors through a sector or industry ETF, or using a country ETF where the country market cap is dominated by a particular sector. For example, a value investor who was concerned about their underweight position in technology, but wanted to avoid exposure to U.S. tech companies, could consider investing in a Taiwan ETF, which would provide a high level of non-U.S. tech leverage. Again, when making one bet—a style bet—consider how it impacts your other risk factor exposures.

INTERNATIONAL INVESTING

The final category of equity risk factors to discuss is the country or regional exposure. Arguably, this area of ETFs is potentially the most useful for individual investors, as it opens up whole new geographies to investing. There are scores of funds organized by both country and region that allow investors to cheaply access both developed and emerging international markets. Expanding into new geographies is one of the easier ways to add diversity to a portfolio.

One mistake most investors, both professional and individual, make is to adopt what is known as a "home country bias." This is a tendency to disproportionately weight your portfolio holdings to your native market. Historically, this was more by necessity, as international investing was often difficult and limited by regulatory and logistical frictions. However, as world markets have expanded and liberalized over the past several decades, there is now little excuse for this bias other than inertia. As large as the United States is, it is still only a minority portion of the world's economy and financial markets. In 2007 the United States represented roughly 20 percent of world GDP, and about 30 percent of the world's stock market capitalization. Why then do most investors, even institutional investors, have the overwhelming majority of their portfolio tied to U.S. assets? While there is a comfort to holding U.S. securities, given both the strong property rights and the familiarity with the companies and climate, investors need to broaden their geographic focus toward Europe, Asia, Latin America, and emerging markets. As many people have become more comfortable traveling to more exotic locations, they need to adapt that same mind-set to their portfolios. Exchange traded funds make it considerably easier to lessen the myopia of the home country bias.

When looking to expand geographically, how should investors approach international markets? Similar to the way we looked at industries and sectors, international diversification can be broken into different levels of granularity. There are regional funds and then there are country-specific funds. This raises the question: how fine or broad do you want to cut your exposure? As with sectors, there are various layers of granularity you can employ when investing in international equities. You can invest based on specific countries, geographic regions, or themes. Specific-country ETFs are self-explanatory, and were one of the first types of exchange traded funds to be launched. Several of the largest and most popular ETFs fit into this category. The second type of international funds includes those devoted to a particular region. This group comprises funds that have a geographic focus such as Latin America, Asia, or Europe. Similar to the sector funds, they offer a broader, more diversified exposure than the country-specific funds. If you felt that Asia offered superior growth prospects, but had little insight into which countries in the region were best situated, you would probably be better off considering an Asian- or Pacific Rim–focused product than a particular country fund. Finally, there is a group of internationally focused ETFs, which I will refer to as thematic. These funds ignore geographic location and focus on broad similarities, such as companies from countries designated as emerging markets.

There are several dozen exchange traded funds focusing on country exposure. Many of the country funds are iShares sponsored by Barclays Global Investors. Traditionally, most of the funds have been focused on what are known as developed markets. This group would include most countries in Western Europe, Canada, Japan, and select countries in Asia and the Pacific such as Hong Kong, Singapore, and Australia. These funds are primarily based on the MSCI benchmark for that particular country. MSCI stands for Morgan Stanley Capital International Inc., and is one of the leading providers of financial indices. Fees for this group of funds are modestly higher than those for the domestically oriented index funds, ranging from 0.50 percent to 0.60 percent of the fund's assets. As a rule of thumb, fees for international beta, even those of large, developed countries, will generally be higher than those for products focusing on domestic beta.

Another point on the beta is that investors should realize that the indices they are purchasing are dominated by large-cap names. This is partly a function of the fact that many foreign markets are more concentrated than those in the United States. A relatively small number of names can make up a large percentage of the overall market cap of that index. For example, look at the German ETF (EWG): the top ten names in that fund make up more than 60 percent of the index.[6] Investors should generally assume that when they purchase a country ETF, they are adding to their large-cap exposure.

A second consideration in regional allocations is the impact they will have on your overall sector weightings. Sector weightings in other countries may differ dramatically from those in the United States. If you have a well-diversified international portfolio, this is not likely to be an issue, as extreme sector weightings in one country will be balanced out by different weightings in other countries. However, if you decided to take a large position in Hong Kong, you should be aware that you've also effectively taken a large position in financial stocks. The Hong Kong iShares (EWH) currently has a 53 percent weighting to financials. Most of that overweight is concentrated in banks and real estate, with most of the top ten holdings of the fund in one of those two categories.[7] Given the fact that the Hong Kong dollar is linked to the U.S. dollar through a currency board, Hong Kong monetary conditions are directly tied to U.S. monetary policy. In that way, despite the geographic distance between the two countries, the performance of Hong Kong financial shares, particularly banks, is not unaffected by the same factors that impact U.S. financial shares. As financials are also currently the largest sector weighting in the United States, more than 21 percent, a large position in Hong Kong would create a significant overweight in global financial stocks.

This problem is not limited to Hong Kong financials, as several foreign markets are dominated by large weightings to one sector or industry. The iShares MSCI Australian Index Fund (EWA) also has large weighting to financials, nearly 50 percent. Invest in an ETF focused on Taiwan, and you're going to get a healthy chunk of technology exposure. The iShares MSCI Taiwan Index Fund (EWT) has nearly 60 percent of its weight in technology, with approximately one seventh of the fund in just one semiconductor stock, Taiwan Semiconductor.[8] These large sector weightings are not a result of the idiosyncrasies of the fund construction, but rather reflect the realities of many of these markets. Given these realities, an important consideration in investing in single-country exchange traded funds is to know the underlying holdings. How much of a given fund's market cap is composed of a small group of stocks or one sector? Given some of the above examples, depending upon your other holdings, a large country bet can easily tilt your portfolio toward an unintended sector bet.

This issue of concentration is particularly acute for those country funds that focus on emerging markets (Taiwan is technically listed as an emerging market, but it is actually one of the larger and more developed ones). ETFs in this category would include all of Latin America, South Africa, and most Asian countries. In general, these countries will be higher risk, but also offer the potential for greater return, as most of them have higher growth rates than developed countries (remember from chapter 1 that long-term earnings growth is linked to GDP potential; generally, emerging-market countries have higher growth rates than more developed ones). The higher potential return does come with higher risk. In addition to the ongoing issues of property rights, geopolitical risk, and corporate governance, the relative concentration of these markets can leave investors effectively leveraged to a very small number of stocks. The iShares MSCI Mexico Index Fund (EWW) has more than 40 percent of its assets in two stocks. One other consideration—fees in these funds tend to be still higher than those of funds that invest in more developed countries. Many of the funds in this category can carry management fees between 0.70 percent and 0.80 percent.

Just as one solution for a concentrated industry bet is a broader sector allocation, regionally oriented exchange traded funds can alleviate some of the drawbacks of country-specific funds. ETFs based on a region offer a broader geographic mandate than single-country funds. The diversity of holdings lowers the country-specific risk associated with the regional ETFs. Again, going back to the early chapters that emphasized focusing your investments to get the exact beta you want, if you want exposure to Europe, you can get that directly without incurring the country-specific risk of investing solely in France. There are currently a number of funds in this category, focusing primarily on Europe, Asia, and Latin America, including:

- iShares MSCI Pacific Rim ex-Japan Index Fund (EPP)
- iShares MSCI EMU Index Fund (EZU)
- iShares S&P Europe 350 Index Fund (IEV)
- iShares S&P Latin American 40 Index Fund (ILF)
- DJ STOXX 50 ETF (FEU)
- Vanguard Pacific ETF (VPL)

The regional funds, by definition, will include companies from more than one country. For example, the Pacific Rim iShares (EPP) includes the four developed countries within the Pacific ex-Japan markets: Hong Kong, Singapore, New Zealand, and Australia. The EMU Index Fund (EZU) tracks companies within all the countries in the European Monetary Union. As these funds cover multiple countries, they tend to have fewer securities per country, and as a result tend to be dominated by large companies. They also tend to have slightly lower management fees than the country-specific funds. For the most part, these funds have annual management fees of between 0.50 percent and 0.60 percent per year. In one case, the FEU, which focuses on European megacap names, the management fee is only 0.30 percent.

While regionally focused exchange traded funds offer a cheap way to gain broad international exposure, there is a trade-off. One of the issues to consider when evaluating a regional exchange traded fund is how homogeneous the region is. For example, an investor looking to gain exposure to the rising "Tigers" of Asia might look elsewhere than the Pacific ex-Japan ETF. In addition to developed markets with arguably slower long-term growth rates, they are also getting a mix of very different countries within that fund. There is a very heavy weighting toward Australia, a market that tends to be dominated by banks and mining companies. While there is nothing wrong with either, neither the country nor those sectors are closely aligned with the faster-growing markets many now associate with Asian equities.

As with the discussion of sector versus industry funds, a country or regional fund does not offer any intrinsic advantage over the other. Rather, an investor's choice of product should be driven by the specificity of the beta he or she is trying to own. What type of focus is an investor looking for? Again, going back to chapter 2, it is helpful to think like an institutional investor. What is the investment theme to which you are trying to gain exposure? Is it country specific, or does it have a broader regional theme? If it is a broader theme, do the available instruments adequately capture that theme, and if so, to what other risks do they expose you? If you are looking for very specific beta, then country exchange traded funds offer a very efficient way to gain access for most investable markets. If your goal is to invest in a broader theme, such as the long-term growth prospects in Latin America, than purchasing a regional fund may be a more elegant way to gain exposure and minimize the country-specific risks you may want to avoid.

There is a third type of international ETF that focuses on more thematic investing rather than geographic specificity. The themes range from emerging markets, which can include countries from South Africa to Malaysia, to growth- and dividend-oriented companies. The common thread is that the funds tend to focus on a particular type of exposure, such as growth, and find international companies that embody that exposure regardless of where they are located. Some examples of funds in this category include:

- iShares MSCI Emerging Markets Index (EEM)
- SPDR S&P Emerging Markets ETF (GMM)
- Vanguard Emerging Markets ETF (VWO)
- iShares MSCI EAFE Value Index Fund (EFV)
- iShares S&P Global 100 Index Fund (IOO)
- iShares MSCI EAFE Growth Index Fund (EFG)
- PowerShares International Dividend Achiever Portfolio (PID)
- WisdomTree Emerging Markets High-Yielding Equity Fund (DEM)

As these funds tend to offer more creative and idiosyncratic exposures, it is worth investigating the underlying holdings. In some instances, different nuances in the index have a relatively minor impact, but in others the differences can be significant. Both the iShares Emerging Markets fund and the Vanguard Emerging Markets fund purport to provide exposure to emerging markets. Yet they use different index constructions, which results in some important differences in holdings. For example, the largest holding in the iShares product is a Korean steel manufacturer, Posco, which has a weighting of roughly 4 percent in the fund. The same stock is ranked only thirteenth, with less than 1 percent, in the Vanguard product. Yet despite this and other similar differences, the two products have a very high correlation. Using more than two years of weekly data, the two funds share a 0.97 percent correlation of returns.

Why would two funds with somewhat different holdings produce very similar returns? Primarily because investors often view emerging markets as a monolith, and tend to trade stocks in the group according to their broader view on the country or region, rather than always on the company-specific fundamentals. For that reason, despite the geographic differences, many of these stocks tend to trade with a very high correlation to one another. As a result, the differences in weightings have a less pronounced impact on the pattern of returns.

Now there are instances where modest differences in two funds' composition can exert a significant impact on performance. In the above example, for the period under discussion, both emerging markets and commodity stocks have performed well. However, under different economic conditions the two themes could diverge. In an environment where global growth was slower, growth-oriented markets are likely to outperform those leveraged to value, particularly so called Old Economy value, such as material or energy stocks. In that type of an environment, an ETF that had larger exposure to the commodity-driven emerging markets Russia and Brazil would be likely to underperform one leveraged to the emerging economies of Asia, which tend to be net importers of materials and energy. Under this scenario, ETFs that track emerging markets could produce different returns based on their exposure to particular countries and sectors. When investing in the more thematically oriented exchange traded funds, investors should be particularly mindful of the unintended risk factors, such as sector and style.

Another example further illustrates the point. The PowerShares International Dividend Achiever Portfolio (PID) provides access to global stocks with a high dividend yield. While an investor may be looking to buy this fund purely for the income, most are unlikely to be indifferent to the capital appreciation. High-dividend-yielding stocks tend to be concentrated in value industries, such as financials, utilities, and telecom. Many of these these industries also share what are known as defensive characteristics, in that they tend to perform relatively better during times of geopolitical tension or economic duress. So a fund that focuses on high-dividend-paying stocks will by definition have a high concentration in these industries. This suggests that during periods of strong economic growth or during regimes when investors prefer more growth-oriented names, a dividend fund is likely to underperform the broader market averages. There may still be a rationale for including this or a similar fund in your portfolio, but it is useful to understand the secondary risk exposures (sector biases) you are taking on along with the higher dividend yield.

One final risk that investors need to be aware of is the currency risk. When an investor purchases an exchange traded fund invested in international securities, he or she is also taking a position on the U.S. dollar. The holdings of international funds, by definition, will be denominated in a currency other than dollars. Unless the fund focuses on a country whose currency is pegged to the dollar, such as Hong Kong, its value will be determined by both the change in the price of the underlying holdings and the change in price of the currency.

Take as an example an investor holding an ETF investing in German securities. Those securities are denominated in euros, which float against the U.S. dollar. Therefore, the return on that fund is partially determined by how the euro is trading against the dollar. If the euro appreciates against the dollar, the U.S. investor will benefit, as the value of those securities will be worth more in U.S. dollars, even if their price in euros does not change. However, if the dollar appreciates against the euro, then the fund's value will decline in dollars, all else being equal. While the change in the prices of the underlying securities is likely to be the primary determinant of performance, as stocks tend to be more volatile than currencies, remember that international holdings also represent a short position on the dollar, and that the value of those holdings will be influenced by the behavior of the currency.

PORTFOLIO CONSTRUCTION: COMBINING THE PIECES

The first part of this book focused on the difficulties of reliably creating alpha. Individuals have consistently found it elusive, while professionals appear to be able to garner it only to the extent that they can cover their own fees. I ended the first part of the book with a strong suggestion to consider an almost semipassive approach: rather than attempting to outperform a benchmark, seek the full benefits of diversification. While sector rotation and country timing require a skill level on a par with stock picking, there is a benefit to be gained by long-term exposure to fast-growing markets. In addition, ETFs can be used to tweak the risk characteristics of your portfolio. If your existing portfolio is underweight to certain sectors or styles, such as growth, exchange traded funds can be an efficient mechanism for adjusting that exposure. Finally, if an investor has a long-term horizon, adding a moderate exposure to faster-growing emerging markets is likely to raise the overall return on the portfolio, as these economies tend to enjoy higher growth rates than more developed countries.

As discussed earlier, international investing offers diversification away from one's home market. At certain times, the benefits will seem small, as country returns can converge, particularly when markets are volatile. However, over the long term, economies can and do follow different cycles, and having a significant exposure away from one's home country is the best way to ride out those cycles. Given the growing diversity of exchange traded funds, they are in many ways the ideal tool for gaining broad exposure to different markets. This is critical, as most domestic stocks will share some positive correlation with the overall market indices. Even if you build a portfolio that is diversified in terms of sectors and styles, you are still subject to the market risk. As discussed in chapter 3, that risk is the price for exposure to returns above the risk-free rate. While market risk is unavoidable, risk associated with a particular country or geography is not. As exchange traded funds provide an easy opportunity for international diversification, domestic-only investing is becoming an increasingly myopic and unnecessary constraint.

International holdings provide diversification across several dimensions. First, it is one methodology to address the synchronicity of most U.S. stocks to the economic cycle. While certain types of stocks, such as utilities or consumer staples, are likely to hold up better under a recession or bear market, this is relative. Utility stocks may go down less than the market during a pullback, but if they have a positive beta, they are still likely to decline as investors sell their holdings of U.S. securities. In contrast, at least some international economies are likely to be in a different stage of their economic cycle, which tends to be closely tied to financial cycles. Diversifying away from one economy helps provide insulation from country-specific events, whether economic, political, or of some other nature.

To the extent there is a global recession, or a single exogenous event such as 9/11, international markets are likely to converge. Under these instances global diversification will offer little benefit, and the only protection is a lack of any equity exposure. However, over the long term, markets are often out of sync, and economies are in different stages of expanding or contracting. Having exposure to different countries and different regions provides a significant benefit. Investors can gain that exposure through a combination of regional and country ETFs. For certain regions, such as Europe and Asia, it is possible to build a diversified set of exposures through a collection of country-specific funds. For other regions, notably Latin America, a regional fund may provide better exposure as not all the countries in that region are represented by a liquid fund.

Diversifying outside of your home country also carries another benefit. Countries can, and occasionally do, go through secular bear markets that can last for decades. During these periods, markets can stagnate. As discussed in the first chapter, the financial conditions of the past quarter century are atypical. There have been extended bear markets in the United States, and in other countries, that have lasted for prolonged periods of time. Between 1968 and 1982, the U.S. equity market barely moved. While there were several periods of strong bull markets, they were invariably followed by equally dramatic bear markets. During this period, an investor in U.S. securities had to make do with the dividend yield on stocks, which for much of that period was below the inflation rate. Effectively, for a period of fourteen years, U.S. investors received no return on an inflation-adjusted basis. In a similar vein, investors who purchased

Japanese stocks at their peak in 1989 have yet to see that market come close to eclipsing its late-eighties highs. An investor who solely focused on either of those markets during the respective time periods would be sorely disappointed with the returns on his or her portfolio.

Even though equities typically offer the best long-term inflation-adjusted returns, secular bear markets do occur with a disturbing frequency. They are particularly likely following periods marked by premium valuations, for example, the United States in 2000 or Japan in 1989. During these secular bear markets, an investor who limits his or her investable universe to the domestic market has few alternatives for generating positive risk-adjusted returns. Including a diversity of regions and countries helps lower the odds of prolonged periods of stagnation. While the Japanese market headed south for a dozen years, stocks in the United States plowed ahead during the period from 1989 to 2000. And while the S&P 500 is only now regaining its 2000 high after seven years of flat performances, other markets, notably in emerging countries, have produced stellar returns.

This home-market bias is a function of psychology (investors feel more comfortable investing in stocks closer to home) coupled with the previous difficulties in gaining access to international stock markets. Thankfully the latter obstacle has now been removed. Regardless of the instruments used, the country, or the region, investors should consider allocating a significant portion of their assets to global markets. Investors now have the opportunity to gain exposure to most international markets, both emerging and developed, in a cost-efficient manner. Given the diversifying benefit of international markets, adding these funds to your portfolio is as close to a free lunch as investors are likely to get in investing.

Continuing with the notion of diversification, there is another way to incorporate exchange traded funds, both domestic and international, into your portfolio. ETFs, particularly the international sector funds, can be used to balance out sector imbalances. Take the previous example of Hong Kong. You may want to include a Hong Kong fund in your portfolio, but in addition to gaining the country-specific exposure, you are also tacitly adding to your global weight in financials, particularly banks and real estate. Including a sector fund in your portfolio is one method for balancing out your sector weights. Perhaps the Hong Kong ETF left your portfolio very underweight in technology. Adding a global sector fund focused on technology may help bring the portfolio weights back into line.

This may be a particularly acute problem during periods when investor preference for one sector becomes disconnected from economic fundamentals. At their peak in 2000, not only were technology stocks trading at unprecedented levels relative to their earnings, of which there often were none, but they were also a disproportionately large portion of the overall U.S. market. By 2000, relentless multiple expansion pushed technology's portion of the U.S. large-cap market up to 35 percent. That meant that an investor focused on U.S. large-cap stocks had nearly one third of his or her portfolio dedicated to technology issues, even though tech was only one of ten economic sectors. An investor who wanted to keep his or her U.S. exposure but was concerned about the concentration of technology could have used one or more ETFs to gain better diversity. At the peak of the bubble, many Old Economy industries, as they were then derisively referred to, were out of favor. Yet investors who used ETFs to raise their portfolio weights to industrials, materials, or energy would have been well rewarded after the bubble burst.

Different sector funds would have had a diversifying benefit, and cushioned the fall in their portfolio when tech eventually began to sell off later that year. This is not Monday morning quarterbacking. Sector weightings at the peak of the bubble were an excellent example of a distortion in a portfolio. An investor whose equity holdings were leveraged to U.S. large-caps would have had a ridiculously heavy position in one sector. Without any forecast on the outlook for technology, a simple plan of diversification would have suggested raising the weights of the other sectors to bring overall holdings back into line. Just to put the above point in context, an investor who bought large-cap U.S. technology stocks in January of 2000 had still lost approximately 50 percent of his or her investment seven and a half years later. By comparison, an investor in the energy and materials sectors gained 150 percent and more than 70 percent, respectively, without dividends, over the same time period.

So far, the discussion of ETFs in this chapter has focused mostly on the diversification benefits. ETFs are a useful vehicle for helping to guarantee adequate sector, style, and country diversification. For individuals willing to be a bit more aggressive, exchange traded funds also provide a vehicle for adding to their exposure in faster-growing market segments, such as emerging markets. These markets do offer the prospect for better long-term earnings growth, as well as currency appreciation. For investors able to tolerate the increased risk, increasing their exposure to emerging markets may add incremental returns over the long term.

The major benefit of these markets is their potential for higher long-term economic growth. This pattern has been evident in recent years, particularly in Asia. Countries in this region, which include Korea, Taiwan, China, India, Thailand, Malaysia, Indonesia, the

Philippines, and Pakistan, have enjoyed accelerating economic growth in the recent past. Asia has been the fastest-growing segment of the world over the past ten years, with the region contributing 50 percent of the world's economic growth. Much of that growth has been driven by the region's continuing integration into the world's economy. These economies tend to be open to trade, and have disproportionately benefited from globalization. Asia's percentage of world trade now stands at nearly 30 percent.[9]

Given that many of these countries also enjoy a better demographic profile than the developed world (i.e., a larger proportion of working-age to retirement-age citizens), many economists would expect their superior growth rates to maintain themselves for several decades. A study by Goldman Sachs several years ago outlined the case for the largest of the emerging market countries, the so-called BRIC economies—Brazil, Russia, India, and China. The study makes the case for a significant shift in the state of the world's center of economic gravity. While the United States is likely to maintain its economic supremacy for a number of decades, many of the other developed countries will see their relative economic position drop in relation to the rising development of these emerging markets. The report goes on to highlight how a combination of higher real growth rates and currency appreciation will push many emerging economies into the top of the league tables by 2050. The expectation is that in less than forty years, BRIC economies could be larger than the G6 (United States, European Union, Australia, Japan, India, and Brazil) in U.S. dollar terms. By 2025 they could account for more than half the size of the G6. Currently, they are worth less than 15 percent. Of the current G6, only the United States and Japan may be among the six largest economies in U.S. dollar terms by 2050.[10]

Nor are these projections founded solely on wide-eyed assumptions about future growth or economic miracles. The growth rates and assumptions on currency appreciation are very much in line with those realized by other countries at a similar stage of development. Had investors had the opportunity or instruments to invest in Japan in the 1950s and '60s, they also could have looked forward to several decades of superior growth and long-term appreciation of the yen against the U.S. dollar. Between 1955 and 1985, real GDP increased by nearly eight times in Japan. At the start of that period, income per capita was at similar levels to several of today's BRIC countries. Over the same period, real industrial production rose tenfold. At the same time, the Japanese currency appreciated by more than 300 percent against the U.S. dollar. Nor was this rate of ascension purely a function of the Japanese economic miracle. During a more recent period, 1970 to 2000, Korea's GDP increased by nearly nine times. Compared to these growth rates, the assumptions inherent in the Goldman Sachs analysis are somewhat conservative.[11]

None of the above should be interpreted as a caution-to-the-wind, unqualified endorsement of emerging markets as the core of a portfolio. These markets do come with increased geopolitical risk and corporate governance issues. The fact that these countries are in an earlier stage of development implies higher volatility as well as faster growth. For that reason, while a high allocation to international stocks is likely to be desirable for most investors, the portion dedicated to emerging markets should be relatively modest, perhaps 5 to 15 percent of the equity exposure. Given the volatility of many of these markets, for most investors without particular insights into a specific country, investing in a thematic ETF such as the EEM or VWO is the best way to gain emerging market exposure.

Characteristics of Equity ETFs

SECTOR ETFS

- How granular is the fund—sector or industry?
- How is the benchmark constructed?
- What weighting scheme is used to determine the stock weights?

STYLE ETFS

- Is the focus market capitalization or value?
- How does the sponsor define the style?

INTERNATIONAL ETFS

- How granular is the fund—country, region, or thematic?
- If it is thematic or regional, which definition is used?
- Is there currency exposure?

Ideally an allocation to emerging markets will provide a double benefit. First, you are including markets in different stages of development with very different economic characteristics (for instance, Russia and Brazil are leveraged to commodity production, with China exposed to global manufacturing and India excelling at the service economy). Second, beyond the diversification benefits they offer higher long-term growth prospects. Should these countries follow similar trajectories to others that have made the transition into developed countries, they are likely to enjoy several decades of superior growth and above-average performance.

Putting it all together, the guidelines for building an equity portfolio are the same regardless of the instruments you use. First and foremost, focus on diversification. When building a diversified equity portfolio, try to think in multiple dimensions such as sector, style, and geography. Pay as little as possible for beta, and at all costs avoid beta masquerading as alpha. Finally, to the extent that you can accept additional risk, consider a modest exposure to emerging markets where higher long-term growth rates are likely to produce higher longer-term returns. Finally, remember the lessons of chapter 2: Consider the bets you are making and where you take on risk. If you don't have superior information, avoid taking excessive positions in markets where you accept greater risk without the prospect for higher returns. In the absence of any insights, make diversification your only priority.

Chapter 6

FIXED-INCOME FUNDS

After equities, the second-largest allocation in most portfolios is fixed-income. Fixed-income securities offer several benefits, the first of which is higher current income. With the potential exception of REITs, and occasionally utilities, fixed-income instruments generally offer higher current income than just about any equity security. In addition, they dampen the volatility of the overall portfolio, as the return on bonds and other similar instruments is generally less volatile than equity securities. Finally, like equities, fixed-income markets are broad and deep. Over recent years, the number and diversity of the fixed-income market has grown substantially. As of 2005, the fixed-income market in the United States was valued at roughly $26 trillion, twice the size of equities. The market has expanded exponentially in recent years, due to a combination of releveraging of corporate balance sheets and the introduction of a host of new instruments.[1] Even the value of $26 trillion stated above significantly understates the magnitude of the size and recent growth. If the value of associated derivative contracts is included, the market looks still larger.

Not only do fixed-income securities dwarf equities in terms of total market size, but in many respects it is a more diverse and complicated market. There is a greater proliferation of instruments, with different purposes and risk characteristics. In order to better understand the fixed-income market, it is useful to divide it into different segments or clusters, as follows:

- Municipal bonds
- Treasuries
- Mortgage-backed securities
- Corporate
- Fed agencies
- Money market
- Asset-backed securities

As of early 2007, about half of these categories were represented by one or more exchange traded funds. The most developed segments are the Treasuries and the corporate markets. Both of these categories have several funds covering varying maturities and, in the case of the corporate market, different credit ratings. There is also a fund covering mortgage-backed and agency securities. The most recent entrants in the space are several new funds based on municipal bond indices. In the fall of 2007 State Street, Barclays Global, and PowerShares all launched municipal funds. These new ETFs are based on national, New York, or California bond indices. As of this writing, all the funds are still in their infancy, with most trading with $25 million or less in AUM. The largest of the group is Barclays iShares S&P National Municipal Bond Fund (MUB), with more than $200 million in assets. The fund tracks the S&P Municipal

Bond Index, which is made up of a portfolio of state and local municipal issues that are exempt from both federal and the federal alternative minimum tax. The ETF carries a .25 percent expense ratio.

FIXED-INCOME RISK FACTORS

Just as was the case in equities, when constructing a fixed-income portfolio it is useful to think in terms of certain risk factors. Just as sector, style, and country/region are the primary risk factors distinguishing equity securities, the bond market has its own unique set of risk factors that are idiosyncratic to fixed-income investments. The two principal ones to be aware of are duration and credit risk. Exchange traded funds can be used to increase or target exposure to particular segments of the maturity or risk spectrum without having to select individual securities, which, as was the case with equities, can carry their own idiosyncratic risks. For example, if you wanted to increase your exposure to the high-yield market there are now several funds that provide that beta. These funds allow you to raise your allocation to the high-yield market without accepting the specific credit risk of one particular issuer.

Let's focus first on credit risk. This is the risk associated with an issuer's ability to repay principal and make the appropriate interest payments. Generally, government bonds, particularly those of the United States, are considered to have the lowest credit risk. That is because they are backed by the full faith and credit of the U.S. government. Corporate bonds have credit risk specific to their issuer, which is in turn a function of the company's debt structure and financial condition. The credit risk of a particular fixed-income security is generally denoted by its rating, which is normally provided by rating agencies such as Moody's or Standard & Poor's.[2] As with equities, there is a positive relationship between risk and return, at least return defined as the yield to maturity on a particular bond. The higher the risk of a particular issue, the higher the interest rate is likely to be. Marginally higher interest rates compensate investors for the increased risk of a default for that particular issue.

The second risk factor specific to the fixed-income universe is the maturity, or more specifically the duration, of the issue. *Maturity* refers to the amount of time until the issuer is scheduled to repay the principal on the bond. A more technical definition of maturity is the bond's duration. *Duration* is a quantitative measure that takes into account not only the time to maturity, but also the size of the coupon payments relative to the principal as well as their timing.[3] One way to think about duration is the time-weighted average of the cash flows. For two bonds with the same maturity date, the one with the smaller coupon payments relative to the principal would have the longer duration. Small coupon payments cause more of the overall cash flow to occur at maturity. As the bond's maturity is farther away than any of the intermediate interest payments, this has the effect of lengthening the bond's duration.

Longer duration coincides with additional risk. There are two reasons for this. First, longer periods until maturity provide more opportunity for the issuer to default on either an interest payment or the principal. Second, longer-maturity bonds are also more at risk to a pickup in inflation. Because inflation erodes the real purchasing power of the principal, inflation is negatively correlated with bond prices. Longer periods until maturity provide more opportunity for unanticipated spikes in inflation.[4] If a bond matures in ten years as opposed to five, there are five additional years during which inflation could increase. As inflationary pressures take time to build, the longer the maturity the more likely the bond holder will experience a significant pickup in pricing pressure.

As with credit, higher duration risk is normally associated with higher returns in the form of higher yields. In most time periods, bonds with longer maturities command higher yields, producing what is known as a positive yield curve (the yield curve charts the yield to maturity of a particular type of bond, such as a U.S. Treasury, across different maturity horizons). There are times, however, when this relationship does not hold, and the curve becomes inverted, meaning that short-term instruments have the same or a higher yield than longer maturities. This condition occurs most frequently when investors are expecting an imminent slowdown in the economy, with an expectation that yields on bonds will soon fall as the economy, and inflation, decelerate. If investors expect future inflation to decelerate, they generally purchase longer-duration bonds. The demand for long-duration bonds pushes prices up and yields down, creating an inverted yield curve (bond prices and yields move in opposite directions, higher prices mean lower yields, and falling prices translate into higher yields). During these periods, investors receive less compensation for the risk of accepting longer durations.

While there are fewer exchange traded funds for fixed-income than there are for equity investments, the market is growing. Over the last few years, sponsors have expanded their list away from Treasuries, which were the first fixed-income ETFs, into corporate bond funds as well as mortgage-backed instruments. In addition, there are also a few new funds that invest in TIPS, a type of U.S.

Fixed-Income Risk

DURATION RISK

Duration measures the sensitivity of bonds or other fixed-income securities to changes in interest rates. The longer the duration of a fixed-income security, the greater its sensitivity to changes in rates.

CREDIT RISK

Credit risk measures the likelihood that the bond issuer will default on an interest and/or principal payment. Debt issued by the U.S. federal government is assumed to have no credit risk. Other issues, such as corporate bonds, have credit risk based on the solvency of the issuer.

---

government bond that provides a hedge against changes in inflation. The proliferation of funds has served to flesh out the exposures of the group to include more of the yield curve and a more varied offering of credit ratings. Not only have the number and types of funds been proliferating, but so have the sponsors. In early 2007, Vanguard, which already had numerous equity-based funds, launched four new fixed-income-oriented funds. Shortly after that, in May of 2007, State Street Global Advisors became the third entry in the fixed-income space with five funds trading on the American Stock Exchange.

TREASURY FUNDS AND DURATION RISK

As the first funds in the fixed-income category were based on various Treasury indices, we will start the discussion there. There are several funds dedicated to the Treasury market, covering most maturities across the yield curve. Generally, these have a relatively low management fee and are liquid and easy to trade. Again, the principal advantage of Treasuries, whether purchased directly or through a fund, is their creditworthiness. Treasuries, like all fixed-income instruments, carry duration risk, but have no credit risk. As these bonds are backed by the U.S. government, there has never been a default of Treasuries. This is not to say that the instruments carry no risk. While an investor in a Treasury can reasonably expect a return of interest and principal, the value of that money will change over time depending upon inflationary pressures. In periods of higher inflation, the purchasing power of any bond will deteriorate and cause the bond to go down in price. While a theoretical investor would get his or her principal back at maturity, the purchasing power of that principal will have diminished. This is to say that while an investor will get back the nominal amount he or she originally invested in the bond, that money will be worth less as inflationary pressure will have pushed up prices in the interim. As discussed previously, the longer the time to maturity, the greater the inflation risk.

Given the primacy of duration as the principal risk factor affecting these funds, they are generally organized according to the maturity of the underlying holdings. The first entrant in the fixed-income category was Barclays Global Investors, which offers several different funds based on the duration of the instruments. All of these instruments are based on the Lehman Index for that duration, and carry a relatively low management fee, normally between 15 and 20 basis points (a basis point being defined as one one-hundredth of 1 percent). On the short end of the curve is the SHY, which tracks the Lehman 1–3 Year Treasury Index. Farther out on what would be considered intermediate duration is the IEI, covering the Lehman 3–7 Year Treasury Index. Also in this category is the IEF, a fund that tracks the Lehman 7–10 Year Treasury Index. Beyond ten years, fixed-income instruments are generally considered to be bonds. There are two other iShares that fall within this category. The TLH tracks the Lehman 10–20 Year Treasury Index, and the TLT provides exposure to Treasury bonds of greater than twenty years to maturity. As mentioned above, Vanguard has also recently added to the number of fixed-income funds. They currently offer a fund for Short-Term Bonds (BSV), two in the Intermediate-Term space (BIV and BND), and one focused on the long end of the yield curve, the Long Term Bond ETF (BLV). Vanguard offers all four funds at a competitively low management fee of 0.11 percent.

State Street Global Advisors is another major sponsor in this space. With the exception of a TIPS offering, the other four funds are, like the BGI funds, based on the Lehman indices. There is a short-term fund, SPDR Lehman 1–3 Month Treasury-Bill (BIL); an aggregate fund, SPDR Lehman Aggregate Bond (LAG); an intermediate fund, SPDR Lehman Intermediate Term Treasury (ITE); and a long-duration fund, SPDR Lehman Long Treasury (TLO). With the exception of the TIPS fund, all trade with a 0.13 percent expense ratio. The final entry, the TIPS ETF (IPE), is based on the Barclays U.S. Government Inflation-Linked Index. This fund trades with a slightly higher expense ratio (0.18 percent) than the others.

Which duration to select depends upon several factors, not the least of which is what other fixed-income instruments are already in your portfolio. If you currently have long-term bonds, the fixed-income ETFs can be used to shorten the duration of the portfolio and lower your risk of unexpected inflation. On the other hand, for a portfolio that is mostly in cash or other short-term instruments, the ETFs linked to the longer-term indices can help to lengthen the duration of your portfolio by adding longer-maturity assets. Those individuals just starting to build the fixed-income section of their portfolio are best advised to have several funds that provide exposure to different parts of the curve, a strategy known as "laddering." An alternative strategy, known as a "barbell" approach, entails holding very short duration paper coupled with very long term duration bonds.

The relevant drawbacks and benefits of the different fixed-income strategies are complex and could easily fill a book of their own. For the purposes of including these funds in your portfolio, the basic points are not dissimilar from the discussion of risk in equity securities—balance your risk and avoid taking any unintended bets. If you don't have any preconceived opinion or information on interest rates or inflation, make sure the fixed-income portion of your portfolio is balanced in terms of duration. A portfolio with too short of a duration is taking a bet on rising inflation, while one with too long of a duration implies a long-term bet on falling inflation. If you are agnostic on the outlook for inflation and rates, keep the maturity of your fixed-income portfolio diversified throughout the curve.

As described above, the principal risk to Treasury securities is the risk that inflation may erode the purchasing power of your bond or note. Bonds are generally more exposed to unexpected inflation than equities, as their payments are fixed. Higher inflation does hurt equities by raising their cost structures, as both wage costs and those for raw materials rise. In addition, higher inflation may also induce the Federal Reserve to raise interest rates, which usually has the effect of dampening both consumer and business demand. However, in other respects, most companies also benefit from some inflation.

A modest amount of inflation has been shown to shore up pricing power and corporate earnings. When inflation is too low, companies have difficulty raising prices, and corporate earnings growth tends to be slower. Certain types of firms, notably in the materials sector, actually do best in an inflationary environment, as commodity prices tend to rise fastest in these regimes (actually the best asset in an inflationary environment is the commodity itself—more on that in the next chapter). So while inflationary environments are not ideal for stocks, there are some offsetting benefits that mitigate the negative impact of higher borrowing costs and rising wages. In contrast, inflation always erodes the purchasing power of a fixed-income instrument, precisely because the instrument's payments do not adjust to the inflationary pressure.

That said, there is a type of fixed-income security that can act as a hedge against inflation, while providing the same credit protection as other Treasury securities. It is known as TIPS—Treasury Inflation-Protected Securities—and it is a relatively new form of Treasury security. What makes TIPS special is a provision that resets the principal in accordance with changes in inflation. The primary advantage of TIPS is that it provides a direct mechanism that protects the holder against unexpected spikes in prices, thereby making TIPS, unlike ordinary bonds, an excellent hedge against inflation.

The first TIPS were floated by the Treasury back in 1997, with the first ETF on TIPS following six years later.[5] As stated above, the principal, the amount originally invested, is periodically adjusted in accordance with changes in the Consumer Price Index, or CPI. The CPI is one of many government statistics designed to track economic conditions. This particular measure is meant to reflect changes in prices at the consumer level. The change in the CPI from month to month provides a proxy for overall inflationary pressures in the economy. TIPS holders receive semiannual coupon payments, the interest on the bond, with the coupon payment calculated based on the adjusted principal.

The net impact of this adjustment is that, unlike other bonds, owners of TIPS are protected against rising inflation. As the principal amount resets, the amount paid at maturity rises at a level commensurate with the level of inflation. The more inflation, the higher the adjustment and the more principal paid back at maturity—in other words, the government pays you more when the bond matures than it cost you when you purchased it. In this manner, the nominal amount received by the investor when the bond matures can be larger than the initial amount paid for the bond. This additional principal will compensate the investor for the lost purchasing power due to inflation. The adjustment also raises the amount of the semiannual interest payments. As the payments are calculated by taking the stated coupon amount, dividing by half, and then multiplying by the principal, a larger nominal principal will also raise the coupon payments. By resetting the principal in accordance with inflation, a holder of a TIPS is insulated from rising prices.

Exchange traded funds based on TIPS offer similar benefits, namely protection against rising inflation. However, there are some subtle differences, mostly concerned with the tax treatment of the funds. Distributions from TIPS holdings are very different from distributions from a TIPS ETF. The TIPS holder receives semiannual coupon payments based on the fixed coupon rate and the adjusted principal. For tax purposes, the principal adjustment is classified as Treasury income, even though it is not distributed to the investor. The coupon payment is also classified as Treasury income. Investors in TIPS must pay tax on the Treasury income that results from the principal adjustment, despite the fact that this incremental income, sometimes known as phantom income, is not paid. In contrast, the 1940 Act structure of an ETF mandates distributions of the principal adjustment as well as the coupon payments on the underlying securities held in the ETF. Therefore, each distribution from an ETF will reflect both coupon payments and principal adjustments.[6]

In an ordinary TIPS, there are two components to the income generated—the coupon and the principal adjustment. However, with an ETF other factors affect the amount of income available for monthly distribution. As a result, the monthly distributions from the TIPS ETF are likely to have more variability than the semiannual coupon payments on an ordinary TIPS. The reason for this is that the ETF income from the principal inflation adjustment is reflected in every month's distribution amount. Income earned from portfolio investments—from both coupon payments and inflation adjustments—is accrued daily based on the accrual type of the bond. However, any cash in the fund is invested in a cash vehicle, and income on the cash will not be considered Treasury income.[7] This is relevant as Treasury income is exempt from state and local taxation, while any income generated from the cash positions will not be.

One other difference between holding a TIPS and an ETF composed of TIPS is worth mentioning. Bonds are often purchased for less or more than their stated principal amount, known respectively as a discount or a premium. If the stated interest, or coupon payment, on a bond is less than the prevailing rate, that bond would trade at a discount, or less than the stated principal amount. Conversely, if the

Fixed-Income ETFs

TOTAL BOND FUNDS

Include long-term bonds, including corporate, Treasury, and mortgage-backed. Examples: iShares Lehman Aggregate Bond Fund (AGG), SPDR Lehman Aggregate Bond (LAG), Vanguard Total Bond Market (BND).

TREASURY FUNDS

Funds carry no credit risk. Key differentiator between funds will be the duration of their holdings. Examples: iShares Lehman 7–10 Year Treasury Bond Fund (IEF), Ameristock/Ryan 10 Year Treasury (GKD), SPDR Lehman Intermediate Term Treasury (ITE).

TIPS FUNDS

These funds hold TIPS which, along with other types of fixed-income securities, offer inflation protection. Examples: iShares Lehman U.S. Treasury Inflation-Protected Securities Funds (TIPS), SPDR Barclays Capital TIPS (IPE).

CORPORATE BOND FUNDS

This category includes funds that invest in both investment-grade and high-yield bonds. The principal differentiator between funds will be the amount of credit risk in their holdings. Examples: iShares iBoxx $ Investment Grade Corporate Bond Fund (LQD), iShares iBoxx $ High Yield Corporate Bond Fund (HYG).

coupon payment is greater than investors could obtain on a new issue, investors will pay an amount greater than the stated principal, and the bond will trade at a premium. There are also some bonds that are issued at a discount or premium to their notional principal amount.

As an ETF TIPS fund will purchase bonds at both premiums and discounts, depending upon the composition of the underlying index, the fund needs a mechanism for adjusting for the difference between the underlying principal amount and the cost of the bond.

When a bond purchased at a premium matures or is sold for less than the premium, there is a capital loss. Likewise, a bond purchased at a discount that is subsequently sold for more, or alternatively matures, registers a capital gain. With a TIPS fund, in order to minimize the capital loss on a premium bond, the fund amortizes premiums on a daily basis for those holdings in its portfolio that were purchased at a premium or were issued at a premium. Premium amortization has a negative income impact for bonds in the portfolio. Bonds purchased at discounts would be treated similarly for the accretion of the discount, enhancing the fund's income. Given the numerous adjustments that are made to the fund's cash flows, it is conceivable that these factors could sum to a negative number. In that event, the fund would not pay a distribution that month, but would carry the negative income amount over to the following month, where it would reduce the following month's payout.[8] The purpose of all of these adjustments is to reconcile the fund's actual cash flows with the accounting nuances of bond premiums and discounts.

CREDIT RISK AND ETFs

Thus far, all of the instruments we have described are funds where the component holdings are backed by the full faith and credit of the U.S. government. With the exception of TIPS, they are all subject to risks associated with unexpected changes in inflation. However, what they lack is any credit risk. There has never been an instance when the federal government of the United States has defaulted on its obligations. It is possible that the government could allow, either intentionally or unintentionally, inflation to accelerate, thereby eroding the purchasing power of its bonds, but even the most paranoid and cautious investors will generally acknowledge that the owner of a Treasury instrument is likely to receive interest and principal on a prompt and reliable basis.

Corporate issuers, on the other hand, offer varying levels of security. Large, well-established corporations with excellent credit offer nearly the security of a Treasury. These bonds pay some modest premium over government-issued debt, and are generally considered safe for conservative investors. Other corporate issuers offer less certain prospects. Corporations have defaulted on both principal and interest, or have changed the terms under which either is paid. As you move across the spectrum of credit quality, companies become more speculative and the amount of interest they pay tends to rise. How much it rises depends largely on economic and market conditions. In periods when investors are risk averse and prize safety over speculation, less financially secure issuers must pay a large premium, in the form of interest payments, to lure investors away from the safety of more secure bonds. At other points, including the middle part of this decade, investors are more aggressive and yield seeking. In these environments they are willing to accept a smaller interest premium, and the spread between lower-quality and higher-quality grades contracts. This spread is known as the credit spread, and is an indication of investors' appetite for risky versus "safer" securities. When purchasing the underlying bonds, or an ETF, investors must evaluate how much compensation they are getting for the incremental credit risk they are assuming. Similar to the situation with equities, higher yields are generally accompanied by higher risk. An investor needs to evaluate not only the level of risk they are seeking, but also, and as important, whether or not they are being adequately compensated for that level of risk.

174 | THE ETF STRATEGIST

Fortunately, there have been several recent additions to the ETF fixed-income menagerie that allow investors a choice of where they want to be on the credit curve. These funds include issues that mix corporate securities and Treasuries, as well as those focused purely on the corporate market. Within the corporate category, the funds are generally delineated into two categories, investment grade and high yield. The bonds rating is based on either Moody's or Standard & Poor's, the two largest rating agencies. Based on Moody's scheme, a bond must carry an investment grade of Baa or higher to qualify. Using Standard & Poor's methodology, the bonds rating must be BBB or better. Those bonds with ratings below this level are considered high yield, or as they are otherwise known, "junk bonds." Securities in this category are considered more speculative and not appropriate for all investors. Moody's ratings of Ba, B, Caa, Ca, and C would qualify as junk, while a rating of BB, B, CCC, CC, or C would signify noninvestment grade on the S&P scale.

Similar to the Treasury funds, most ETFs in the corporate credit category are based on a Lehman index. The broadest fund is the AGG, or iShares Lehman Aggregate Bond Fund (AGG). The fund tracks a broad index of bonds, which includes both Treasuries and corporate securities. The index seeks to track both the yield and performance of the United States investment-grade bond market. Approximately 55 percent of the bonds in the portfolio are government bonds, with most of the remaining 45 percent in corporate securities. While most of the bonds are U.S., there is a small allocation to other countries including Canada. This is a large and liquid fund, with nearly $6 billion in market capitalization. Due to the popularity and liquidity of the index, the fees on this product are low, a 0.20 percent expense ratio. In addition, Vanguard offers two similar funds. The Vanguard Intermediate-Term Bond fund (BIV) is based on the Lehman Brothers 5–10 Year Government/ Credit Index. Similar to the BGI product, this fund mixes both corporate and government bonds with an intermediate-term duration. The Vanguard Long-Term Bond ETF (BLV) also blends corporate and government issues. The difference between the BIV and BLV is that the latter focuses on longer-duration issues, with a maturity of greater than ten years. For investors looking to gain exposure to a pure corporate benchmark, there are a number of funds of varying duration and credit quality. On the investment grade side, there are three offerings from BGI: the iShares Lehman 1–3 Year Credit Bond Fund (CSJ), the iShares Lehman Intermediate Credit Bond Fund (CIU), and the iShares Lehman Credit Bond Fund (CFT). All three of these funds focus on investment-grade corporate issues, with the difference between them being the duration. In the case of the CSJ, the top ten holdings, which make up nearly 50 percent of the weight, all mature within the next three years. The intermediate-term fund, CIU, is primarily invested in bonds with a maturity between three and ten years. The CFT has the most diversified portfolio, with fixed-income instruments throughout the maturity spectrum, although the average duration is longer than either of the other two funds. One cautionary note on these funds—while management fees are low, 0.20 percent, the funds are fairly small. All three are currently less than $100 million.

The Vanguard fixed-income offerings also encompass a mix of Treasuries and investment-grade corporate. In addition, these funds also have a small allocation to international investment-grade paper (another term for securities). The funds all track Lehman indices that mix both government and investment-grade corporate bonds.

The primary difference between the four funds is the maturity. The BSV focuses on short-term fixed-income instruments, with a maturity between one and five years. The BIV comprises government and investment-grade instruments with a maturity of five to ten years, while the bonds in the BLV have maturities of ten years or more. The fourth fund, the BND, tracks the performance of the Lehman Brothers Aggregate Bond Index, which is a broad measure of taxable investment-grade bonds. Despite its relatively short track record, the BND has already accumulated a reasonable amount of assets under management, approximately $1 billion as of this writing.

For those larger investors who are looking for greater liquidity, there is an alternative in the investment-grade space, the iShares iBoxx $ Investment Grade Corporate Bond Fund (LQD). This fund corresponds to the U.S. investment-grade corporate market using the iBoxx $ Liquid Investment Grade Index. This fund, while based on a less-well-known index, is actually much larger than the Lehman-based funds, with nearly $3 billion in market cap (it also has a slightly lower management fee of 0.15 percent). As with the CFT, the LQD comprises a diversified portfolio of investment-grade corporate bonds. No one bond makes up much more than 2 percent of the portfolio.

Moving away from the investment-grade issues, there are also ETFs for those investors who want to gain exposure to the high-yield parts of the bond market. BGI offers an ETF based on another iBoxx index, the iBoxx $ Liquid High Yield Index. The iShares iBoxx $ High Yield Corporate Bond Fund (HYG) invests in speculative, or high-yield bonds, as well as preferred stock (preferred stock is often viewed as a bond proxy, as it offers high current income with little or no opportunity for capital appreciation). Bonds in this fund tend to be intermediate duration, with an average weighted maturity of approximately six years, and duration of approximately 4.5 years. The average yield to maturity of the bonds is currently 7.5 percent. In contrast, the LQD, which invests in investment-grade securities, has an average yield of less than 6 percent.[9]

By moving from the investment-grade to a high-yield product an investor will pick up approximately 1.5 percent in additional interest per year. Now, whether or not that is worth it is dependent upon an investor's degree of risk appetite. However, it is worth pointing out that this spread is fairly low by historical trends, meaning that an investor purchasing a portfolio of high-yield bonds is receiving a relatively small premium in yield for the marginal risk. To some extent this may be justified by the fact that the economy is relatively robust and default rates are low, but investors should remember that high-yield instruments carry more risk than investment-grade ones. As with all of the other choices, an investor needs to evaluate whether the marginal pickup in return is sufficient compensation for the higher risk of default.

As noted above, preferred stock is often viewed as an alternative to bonds. In addition to a high current yield, preferred stock is similar to fixed-income instruments in other ways. As its name implies, preferred stock ranks higher in terms of credit claims on a company's assets than common stock. In addition, the dividend is paid ahead of the common, making it theoretically safer and more stable. The downside is that preferred stocks normally do not offer the upside potential of common, so investors generally view them as a source of income rather than capital appreciation. For that reason, despite being technically equity securities, they are often viewed as part of a fixed-income portfolio. Currently, there are a few funds that focus on preferred shares, the iShares S&P U.S. Preferred Stock Index Fund (PFF) and the PowerShares Financial Preferred Portfolio (PGF). The former is based on the U.S. S&P Preferred Stock Index, and carries a yield roughly between that of the investment-grade and high-yield iShares. The fund is still relatively small, with a market cap of approximately $50 million. It also carries a management fee of 0.48 percent. The PowerShares version carries a slightly higher expense ratio, but it is the larger of the two, with more than $100 million in assets. It is based on a different index, the Wachovia Hybrid & Preferred Securities Financial Index. In general, investors should view both of these products as fixed-income proxies, which, depending upon market conditions, may offer a marginal pickup in yield over and above investment-grade debt securities.

There are other segments of the bond market besides Treasury and corporate securities. There are also municipal bonds, agencies, mortgage- and asset-backed, as well as an ever growing cornucopia of derivative products based on various fixed-income instruments. As of this writing, most of these other types of fixed-income instruments have yet to claim a representative ETF. An exception is the mortgage-backed market, for which there is an iShare ETF, the iShares Lehman MBS Fixed-Rate Bond Fund (MBB). This fund is based on an index of investment-grade agency mortgage-backed securities, represented by the Lehman Brothers U.S. MBS Fixed-Rate Index.

The securities in this fund are primarily the debt of various quasi-government entities such as Fannie Mae and Freddie Mac. Both companies were established by Congress back in the 1970s to buy and hold mortgages, which they finance through the sales of mortgage-backed securities. The corporations were established to help provide liquidity to the U.S. housing market, and to facilitate a liquid market in mortgages. While neither is explicitly backed by the full faith and credit of the U.S. government, the way Treasuries are, most investors treat their debt as implicitly backed by the government, and as a result it tends to be viewed as almost risk free. The MBB invests in the debt of these two entities as well as some of their small cousins such as Ginnie Mae. Virtually all of the debt is rated AAA. The yield on the bonds is generally slightly more than Treasuries, but generally less than investment-grade corporate securities. Also, the duration of the mortgages tends to be relatively short, as mortgage-backed bonds may be subject to prepayment, as some of the underlying mortgage holders pay off their debt ahead of schedule. Because of this, the bonds tend to have shorter durations. The fund carries an expense ratio of 0.35 percent, slightly more than a similar Treasury fund.

In general, investors can think of the mortgage-backed market, as it is currently represented by the MBB, as a marginally riskier security when compared to the Treasury-based ETFs. However, as the marginal pickup in risk is minimal, it is still appropriate for more risk-averse investors who are looking to gain slightly higher yields than they can generally obtain on Treasuries. The choice between mortgage-backed bonds and Treasuries echoes the larger issues that investors face when choosing between fixed-income securities. Whether using exchange traded funds or buying the bonds directly, investing in fixed-income securities is largely a matter of selecting duration and credit quality (there is a broader list of risk factors for more opportunistic professional investors, such as convexity, but they do not factor into the ETF world). When selecting from a list of fixed-income funds, investors need to decide where they want to position this portion of their portfolio in terms of duration and credit.

Moving farther out on the credit spectrum will generally result in higher yields, but at the price of a higher probability of default on either the interest, principal, or both. In deciding where to be, investors should consider three criteria: their own level of risk aversion, how the fixed-income risk relates to the risk in their overall portfolio, and the extent to which they are being compensated for accepting incremental risk. The first factor is straightforward, and not specific to bonds. As discussed at length at the beginning of this book, selecting financial assets is largely centered on the trade-off between risk and return. The more you are willing to risk, the greater your likely return. In this respect, bonds are no different from equities. As increasing the beta of your stock holdings is likely to increase the overall return, accepting more credit risk in the form of lower ratings should have a similar effect.

The second consideration in assessing the credit quality of your portfolio is to examine the choice in a broader context. Ideally, investors should be cognizant of risks that cut across different asset classes. This is particularly true for corporate credit, where similar risks can affect both stocks and bonds. Imagine a portfolio of only two assets: a stock in Company X and a corporate bond issued by the same company. While the portfolio is 50 percent stocks and 50 percent bonds, most would agree it is not diversified. The issues that impact the creditworthiness of the issuer are also likely to impact the earnings on the equity securities. An exogenous event that hurts the company is likely to have a similar effect on all parts of the capital structure, both equity and debt. In a similar vein, if you have a fixed-income portfolio that is leveraged to credit risk, and an equity portfolio that is overweight to financials, you may find that your overall portfolio is too leveraged to financial risks. Factors that affect the credit quality of the U.S. high-yield sector, such as a rise in delinquencies, are also likely to affect the financial stocks you hold. When considering your credit exposure, consider how common factors may impact not just the fixed-income positions but other holdings in your portfolio as well.

Finally, when evaluating where you want to be on the credit curve, consider the marginal return you are getting for your risk. Beta is generally considered to be a linear relationship—take more risks and witness a corresponding increase in returns if the stock or the market rises. Credit is slightly more complicated in that the amount of incremental return may not be linear, suggesting that under certain conditions a good deal more risk may yield little in the way of incremental returns. For example, as of this writing, credit spreads are unusually tight by historical standards. What this means is that investors in high-yield instruments are receiving a much smaller marginal return for accepting lower credit quality than investors who bought similar instruments five years ago. Perhaps this lower return is justified by better fundamentals and a lower risk of default by the issuer. Alternatively, investors may be adopting too sanguine a view of the market, economy, and overall credit quality. Under the latter scenario, these bonds may not be offering an adequate return for the risk that is being accepted. Yields are the fixed income's version of price-to-earnings ratios, as they provide a signaling mechanism for how much good news is already discounted into the security. If a high-yield bond, or fund of bonds, has a narrow spread over an investment-grade security, then the market is factoring in a low risk of default. Otherwise, investors would demand a greater premium to accept the incremental risk. The final point to consider when evaluating where to be on the credit curve is how much margin for error appears discounted into the yield on the fund. The lower the yield, the more the market has already discounted most potential good news.

After investors have selected the credit exposure they want, they need to consider the duration of their portfolio. Choosing the duration of your portfolio entails forecasting future interest rates and inflation, a prediction as tricky to make as picking stocks. Consider the choice facing investors back in the early 1980s. As discussed in chapter 1, new government bonds were paying interest rates in the low teens back in 1982. This was a yield significantly higher than even the stock market's long-term return, with the added benefit that investors were being offered this yield on a risk-free asset (even in the depths of the recession, very few investors expected the U.S. government to default on its debt obligations). Not only were these bonds offering a spectacularly high yield, but that yield was also exempt from state taxes, making it even more attractive. How was it that the government had to offer such a high coupon for its debt at a time when the federal budget deficit was considerably lower than it would be a few years hence? The reason is, at the time, everyone extrapolated the upward trend in inflation and expected prices to continue to accelerate. As such, they demanded a high coupon payment to compensate them for the price erosion they had been conditioned to expect. When Paul Volcker aggressively tightened monetary conditions in the early 1980s, inflation began to decelerate, and has been on a downward trajectory for most of the past quarter century. Anyone who happened to have the foresight to purchase a long-term government bond back in 1982 has done spectacularly well, without having to endure the periodic gyrations of the equity market.

The previous example illustrates the skill, and fortitude, investors need to time interest rates. Most investors lack the prognostication abilities to pick inflection points in inflation, just as selecting the right stocks has proved exceedingly difficult. However, without reading the economic tea leaves, there are some basic tools and techniques that bond investors can employ. These are mostly analogous to the credit-spread method described above. Investors should compare the current yield on a risk-free, that is, Treasury, note or bond with the current inflation rate (for this purpose look at the core rate, which excludes food and energy prices). This spread will give you the current real yield on your fixed-income instrument. Basically, should inflation remain stable over the remaining life of the bond, this is the after-inflation yield the bond would provide. Historically, the U.S. 10-year Treasury note has yielded approximately 2.70 percent above the core inflation rate. This rate is also in line with what most economists view as the true cost of money, which is generally assumed to be somewhere between 2 percent and 3 percent.

If your bond fund has a real yield substantially below 2.7 percent, there are a few explanations. The most obvious would be a soft economy, where the demand for money is very low. In a similar vein, investors may expect inflation to decelerate over the life of the bond. Another potential explanation, one that has intrigued economists and traders in recent years, is that some investors, such as foreign central banks, are indifferent to yields and have other motivations for purchasing U.S. Treasuries, such as maintaining their currencies' exchange rate against the dollar. Whatever the

Fixed-Income Considerations

CREDIT SPREAD

What is the incremental or extra interest received for accepting credit risk? If a fund has securities with credit risk (corporate, mortgage-backed, etc.) what is the marginal pickup in yield when compared with a fund with no credit risk (U.S. Treasuries) and a similar duration?

REAL RETURN

Real return compares the yield-to-maturity on a bond with the current level of inflation. Historically, long-term U.S. Treasuries have yielded approximately 2.70 percent above the inflation rate (note that this number is fairly consistent regardless of which measure of inflation you use). A real yield significantly below this level would suggest that bond investors are expecting an economic slowdown, with an accompanying drop in inflation.

explanation, you should be aware that the real yield you are getting is low by historical standards. Alternatively, a yield substantially above 2.7 percent would suggest an unusually high thirst for capital, or a belief that core inflation was likely to accelerate over the life of the bond. From an investor's point of view, the higher the real yield the better, as it suggests a higher after-inflation return. A high real yield also provides some cushion against an unexpected rise in inflationary pressure. As was the case with credit spreads, the wider the spread, the more margin for error. If real yields are low, and inflation takes an unexpected turn higher, the inflation-adjusted return on your fund will decrease, and even potentially turn negative.

Investing in the fixed-income market entails a different set of risk factors but similar principles to investing in equities. Pay attention to the key betas of duration and credit risk. If you have no insight into future performance, seek to neutralize your exposures by building a portfolio that is diversified to these risk factors. As with equities, focus on instruments that provide that diversification, and avoid unintended exposures. In addition, think about the incremental return you are getting for the risk you are taking. What is the spread between a fund that has default risk and one that does not? How does that spread compare to historical norms? If it is low, are you comfortable with the assumptions the market is making, or is there better value in another segment of the market, such as preferred stock? Similarly, when thinking about duration, consider the real yield on the fund. You don't have to make any forecasts about future inflation or market conditions, but you should at least be aware of what the expectation for inflation is over the maturity of the fund. If the real yield is sufficiently low, it may make sense to invest in TIPS, which offer inflation protection. The bond market has many segments, some of which can be a bit esoteric. But the diversity also offers an advantage. As new funds continue to be created, investors will have increasing choices of where to look for value.

Chapter 7

COMMODITY FUNDS

BENEFITS OF COMMODITIES IN A PORTFOLIO

So far, we have focused on the two main asset classes from which most individuals build a portfolio: stocks and bonds. Both represent securities, or paper assets. Both equities and corporate bonds represent some interest in the capital structure of a listed company. There is another asset class that has become increasingly popular in recent years which is quite different. Commodities represent no interest in a company (equities) or a promissory note from a company (bonds). Instead, they are claims on actual physical assets such as crude oil, precious metals, industrial metals, or agricultural goods. For most of the bull market of the 1980s and 1990s, commodities represented a minute portion of most portfolios, as the long-term secular drop in prices meant a long bear market for most physical assets. The drop in prices was compounded by the fact that, unlike bonds or dividend-yielding stocks, commodities offer no current income.

That has all changed this decade. For the first time since the 1970s, commodities have come back in vogue. As commodity prices have surged, investors have rediscovered the benefits of including them in their portfolios. Oil prices have climbed sevenfold since their lows in the late 1990s. And gold, which was being written off in the 1990s after serving as a store of value for millennia, has also staged a startling comeback. The stunning rise in commodity prices, which also includes base metals and agricultural goods, has reminded investors that inflation is not a one-way ride, and that prices can indeed rise, even when central banks are vigilant. Supporting the argument for a sustained rise in commodities is the fact that much of the recent surge has been demand driven, rather than a function of a supply shock, as was often the case in the past. As a number of emerging-market countries make the transition to developed economies, their thirst for various raw materials has increased. Given the still pronounced difference in living standards between emerging and developed countries, this trend could conceivably last for some time.

In addition to the demand side, there have also been a number of supply constraints that have added to the recent bull market in commodities. This is particularly true within the energy complex. Oil and gas producers are finding themselves going to ever greater lengths to maintain their production. A greater reliance on unconventional hydrocarbons such as tight gas, coal-bed methane, deep-water oil, and tar sands is having the net effect of raising the cost of supply. A more expensive supply curve coupled with increased demand has conspired to keep commodity prices elevated. None of the above prevents commodities from experiencing bear as well as bull cycles. Even secular bull markets have their occasional wobble (think of 1987, 1990, 1997, and 1998 for U.S. equities).

There is another value to commodities besides the long-term secular growth story. In the previous chapter, inflation was described as the bane of bonds, and not particularly good for equities. Both asset classes tend to underperform cash during periods of accelerating inflation. And while there are certain stocks, as well as TIPS, that do well when inflation is rising, the best hedge against accelerating prices is commodities. In that sense, commodities are the opposite play to bonds. While the fixed-income component of bonds makes them more valuable when interest rates and inflation are falling, commodities perform best when inflationary pressure is growing. That is because a bond pays out in fixed amounts of cash. If that cash is worth less because of inflation, the bond is worth less. In contrast, owners of commodities don't own cash, but a physical asset whose price tends to rise with inflation. In that respect, commodities are the perfect inflation hedge.

In addition to their value as a natural inflation hedge, adding commodities to your portfolio provides another advantage as well. As commodities respond very differently to inflationary regimes from stocks or bonds, historically commodities have enjoyed a low or even negative correlation with the other two asset classes (although this benefit has eroded a bit in recent years, as commodity prices have become increasingly correlated with equities).[1] As discussed in the first section of the book, adding assets with negative correlations provides for better diversification and risk-adjusted returns. This relationship holds true for asset allocation as well as stock selection. By combining a modest amount of commodities with equities and bonds, an investor can obtain a higher portfolio return for a given level of risk.

The long-term negative relationship between commodities and other asset classes is well documented. Looking at the period from 1970 to 2003, which included both bull and bear markets in stocks and bonds, commodities shared a negative relationship with both international and domestic stocks as well as bonds. The correlation between the Goldman Sachs Commodity Index (GSCI) and the S&P 500 was −0.27. There was also a negative correlation, albeit of a smaller magnitude, between commodities and international stocks. Finally, the asset class also displayed a negative relationship with bonds and a zero correlation with cash.[2]

One natural question is, if an investor has the flexibility to purchase stocks, or funds of stocks, of commodity producers, why go to the trouble of purchasing the assets directly? Wouldn't a gold mining company or a paper firm provide similar exposure without the need to purchase another asset? The problem with purchasing the stocks, or even getting a fund of commodity stocks, is you are not getting direct exposure to commodities as a risk factor, or beta. Companies have operational and management issues that may distort how their performance tracks the commodity they produce. An even bigger problem is the extent to which producers may hedge their exposure by selling their product in the futures or forward market. This practice has the impact of lowering a firm's dependence on future price. While the company's hedges are in place, their relationship to the commodity price will be very different from periods when they are unhedged. This has the effect of lowering the company's, or industry's, beta to the commodity. Tracking a company's hedges is extremely difficult, as the information may not be reported or is often buried in footnotes. Therefore, having accurate and timely insights into a company's or industry's hedge book is a challenge even for institutional investors. Depending on current industry practices, hedged companies may provide very weak exposure. For this reason, owning the commodity directly is a more efficient and consistent method for gaining exposure to this risk factor.

One of the historical problems with investing in commodities has been how to gain exposure. Even for an investor who wanted to take a punt on copper or oil, it was logistically difficult, particularly for small retail investors. Prior to the last several years, the only way to gain exposure to commodities was to actually buy the physical commodity or purchase a derivative of it. While this was relatively easy for a few commodities such as gold and silver, most investors lacked the physical storage space to store hundreds of barrels of oil, tons of copper, or warehouses full of corn. The other alternative was to purchase a derivative contract, such as futures. These are instruments that provide exposure to an asset, such as a commodity, without having to actually own the asset. Instead, your position, either long or short, is paired against another investor's and guaranteed through a clearinghouse. Unfortunately, trading futures has its own difficulties. Futures contracts are for limited periods of time, and must be periodically renewed. For investors who wish to maintain a long-term strategic exposure to a commodity this can be expensive, as the contracts have to be renewed or "rolled" to a future month. In addition, the brokerage account where you own stocks or bonds may not be licensed to trade futures, necessitating another account with a futures brokerage.

COMMODITY ETFs

As with international investing, exchange traded funds have made it much easier to gain access to these more esoteric betas. Ten years ago, ETFs were about stocks. More recently bonds have been added as well. Now exchange traded funds can provide exposure to a wide array of assets. Over the past several years, several commodity-based instruments have been launched. It is now possible to purchase a fund that offers a broad or targeted exposure to various commodities. Unlike stocks and bonds, which often move in tandem, commodities behave very differently from other asset classes. Commodity prices will often rise when the other two asset classes are falling— think of the 1970s. Having funds that provide easy access to this asset class helps provide another layer of portfolio diversification.

Before proceeding further, it is worth mentioning that some commodity funds are structured very differently from the more typical equity or bond funds. In some instances, they are not funds at all, at least not in the legal sense of the word. Many of the most popular commodity-linked products are based on a legal vehicle known as an ETN, or exchange traded note. Where ETFs represent an ownership interest in the underlying assets, exchange traded notes are senior, unsecured debt securities. The securities obligate the issuer, often a large bank or investment bank, to pay a return based on a designated index. The notes are collateralized by an underlying portfolio of securities. Like exchange traded funds, they trade daily on an exchange.[3] To reiterate, an ETF's price will fluctuate based on the price of the underlying assets owned by the fund. In contrast, an ETN is structured more like a bond, with a promise to pay something. With an ETN, what you own is a note from an issuer that promises to pay you some return based on the performance of an index, for example the price of oil. Your returns will mimic the returns on the commodity, but you do not in effect own the underlying commodity.

There are also some subtle differences between ETNs and ETFs that revolve around their creation and redemption. In addition, investors need to be aware of the credit risk implicit in buying an ETN. Exchange traded notes are registered under the 1933 Securities Act (remember, exchange traded funds are registered under the 1940 Investment Company Act). Because ETNs are debt instruments, there is some risk that the issuing party will not pay. In the case of exchange traded notes, the payment is based on the performance of a particular commodity index, rather than a stated coupon payment. In addition, unlike ETFs, which are open-ended and have no expiration date, these notes come with a term of thirty years, and therefore a fixed maturity.[4]

Returning to the topic of commodity investing, allocations within this space are more straightforward than in selecting between stocks or bonds. Unlike equities and fixed-income securities that require controlling for several risk factors across multiple dimensions, commodity risk can be expressed in one dimension, the type of commodity. Commodities can be grouped into a small list of categories, similar in nature to the sector classifications discussed in chapter 5. These categories combine commodities with similar characteristics and fundamentals. For the purposes of most investors, the existing list of exchange traded funds and notes can provide adequate exposure to both broad-based commodity indices and specific commodities. An example of the former would be an all-inclusive commodity index such as the DJ-AIG Commodity Index. A more focused fund would be one specializing in agricultural, energy, or metals. As we go through the list of existing funds, it will be useful to decompose the products based on the index they are replicating. Subtle differences in composition and weighting can leave investors with very different exposures, so it is worth disaggregating the different indices to gain a deeper understanding of what they actually represent.

Commodity Categories

ENERGY

Includes crude oil, natural gas, and potentially refined products, such as gasoline. Energy commodities are economically sensitive, in that they tend to appreciate when economic prospects are strongest. Crude oil also tends to trade on geopolitical concerns that affect supply.

PRECIOUS METALS

Gold, silver, and platinum. While silver and platinum both have industrial uses, this group, particularly gold, is most affected by inflationary concerns. Gold performs best when investors expect higher inflation and/or a weaker dollar.

INDUSTRIAL COMMODITIES

A broad category that generally includes commodities used in industrial processes and construction. Often weighted toward metals, such as copper, zinc, and aluminum, this category tends to be very cyclical, with performance linked to expectations for economic growth, particularly in the manufacturing sector.

AGRICULTURAL/LIVESTOCK/SOFTS

Depending upon the particular definitions of the different index providers, this category generally includes food, livestock, and soft commodities, such as cotton. Less economically sensitive than other groups, this group is often driven by weather-related issues, particularly in the case of agricultural commodities, such as wheat and corn.

Commodities can be viewed as one monolithic asset class, and as such, there are a number of different indices that combine all of the different subgroups into a single index. These indices include all of the major subcomponents including energy, precious metals, and base or industrial metals, as well as agricultural commodities. While broad indices tend to include different representative commodities from each basket, the exact composition and weight can vary. This is not just a technical point, but one that can be very relevant for investors. Just as different equity sectors have unique characteristics that can respond very differently to various economic scenarios, commodities can differ as well. For example, industrial metals such as copper or aluminum tend to be sensitive to economic conditions. Copper prices in particular tend to be very leveraged to expectations for future economic growth, earning the commodity the nickname "Dr. Copper," as many economists believe that changes in copper prices are a leading indicator of economic activity.

Occupying a similar role for inflationary expectations, gold has historically been viewed as a store of value, and a hedge against both inflation and a depreciating dollar. As such, its fortunes are often tied to expectations for the U.S. dollar (generally gold and the U.S. dollar move in opposite directions). Energy prices, specifically crude oil, have the unique distinction of reacting disproportionately to geopolitical news, particularly when it involves the Middle East. The primacy of OPEC and Middle Eastern energy providers makes crude oil particularly sensitive to potential disruptions in this region. Then there are those commodities that are weather sensitive. This group generally includes agricultural commodities, whose supply is often a function of weather patterns, but can also include natural gas, an energy commodity. Natural gas prices are influenced by extreme cold temperatures, particularly in the northeastern section of the United States. A harsh winter in the Northeast can drive up gas prices as demand tends to be dependent on home heating needs. While commodities generally tend to move together over the long term, short-term patterns can vary depending upon the factors enumerated above. Given the diversity of factors that can affect different commodities, performance can diverge for extended periods of time. When selecting between different products, investors should pay attention to the composition of the index, as different weighting schemes can produce different exposures to many of these commodity-specific factors.

Of the broad commodity indices, the largest fund is the iPath Dow Jones–AIG Commodity Index Total Return ETN (DJP). This is an exchange traded note that is designed to provide performance based on the Dow Jones–AIG Commodity Total Return Index. The instrument, which currently has a market capitalization of more than $2 billion, is designed to produce returns commensurate with a nonleveraged investment in the futures contracts or underlying physical commodities (plus the rate of interest that would be earned on the cash collateral).[5] The fund charges a 0.75 percent annual fee.

The underlying index is composed of nineteen commodities organized into five sectors: energy, industrial metals, agriculture, livestock, and precious metals. The commodities in the index are rebalanced, or adjusted on an annual basis, and the weightings of any one subgroup are capped at 33 percent as of the March 2006 rebalancing (weightings for a particular segment can rise above that level between rebalancing depending upon the performance of the individual commodities).[6] Investors in this fund have roughly 30 percent of their exposure in the energy complex, with the majority of that split evenly between crude oil and natural gas. Industrial metals make up roughly 25 percent of the index, with most of the weight divided between copper and aluminum. Precious metals count for another 10 percent, with most of the exposure to gold. One interesting characteristic of the index is the relatively heavy weighting to agricultural and livestock components. Together, these two sectors account for roughly 40 percent of the fund, a particularly large weight compared to other commodity indices. The commodities in this category include soybeans, corn, wheat, cattle, hogs, soybean oil, sugar, cotton, and coffee.[7]

The heavy weighting in agricultural commodities is important as it affects the sensitivity of the index to general inflationary and economic trends. As discussed above, agricultural and livestock prices are influenced by weather conditions, which affect both acreage planted and harvest (consider the impact of frost on orange crops or excess rain on wheat planting). In addition, agricultural and livestock prices can also be affected by a number of idiosyncratic factors that have no relationship to the overall macroenvironment. An example of this would be the outbreak of mad cow disease in the early part of this decade. For this reason, these commodities tend to have a lower beta or exposure to overall global and domestic economic growth. That is not necessarily a problem, as they provide a diversifying benefit to the asset class. But if an investor wants to purchase a commodity instrument with the explicit intention of leveraging to global growth, or in the belief that overall inflation will accelerate, an index heavily weighted to agricultural commodities may not provide the intended exposure. The practical effect would be that in an environment of gangbuster economic growth, an agriculturally weighted index would be likely to underperform an index weighted more heavily to energy and industrial metals, both of which tend to be more sensitive to overall economic activity.

In addition to the DJP, Barclays also offers an iShares fund based on the GSCI Total Return Index, the GSG. Both trade at a similar fee of 0.75 percent, but the GSG is considerably smaller at roughly $300 million in market cap. The GSG is technically a trust in which investors buy shares. The trust itself holds futures contracts on the

S&P GSCI Excess Return Index. These contracts are continually rolled over to maintain the desired exposure to the index. Cash that is not needed for collateral on the futures is invested in Treasury bills.[8]

Comparing the DJP to the GSG brings home the importance of examining the underlying index on which any ETF is based. It is not that one index is theoretically "right," but that their respective weightings are dramatically different. Two investors, both of whom believe they are long on commodities, could experience dramatically different returns based on which product they owned. In the case of the Goldman Sachs Index, the weightings are much more tilted toward energy-related commodities than in the Dow Jones version. In aggregate, energy accounts for nearly 70 percent of the index, with two thirds of that weight in crude oil. The rest of the energy exposure is made up of natural gas and refined products, such as heating oil and gasoline. Another critical difference is that precious metals compose a relatively small portion of the Goldman Index, with gold and silver accounting for less than 3 percent in aggregate. Also, while agricultural and livestock were a significant weight in the Dow Jones–related product, they are only about 15 percent in the GSG.[9]

In comparison, the GSG is much more energy dependent, and cyclically influenced. With more than 80 percent of its weight in energy and industrial metals, the index will be much more influenced by global economic activity than the more agriculturally weighted Dow Jones Index. Another consideration is that the GSG is likely to be more sensitive to geopolitical events than the DJP. With its heavy weighting to oil in particular, negative news out of the Middle East or Russia is likely to reverberate more significantly with the GSG.

Finally, going back to the theme of thinking about your risk exposures holistically, if you invest in the GSG you should carefully consider what other exposures you have to energy-related securities. Do you have a large overweight position in energy stocks? If so, you may be overconcentrating your portfolio in energy by having multiple exposures across asset classes. This argument holds true for other commodity products as well. Just as a bond investor needs to be aware of common risk factors their fixed-income instruments may share with their equity portfolio, commodity owners should think along the same lines. If you have a large weighting to a single commodity such as oil or metals, what other parts of your portfolio have a similar risk factor? Given the heavy energy concentration of the GSG, it is worth considering whether that concentration magnifies significant risk exposures already present in your portfolio. If so, then a more diversified product, such as the DJP, may be more appropriate. If, on the other hand, you are looking to get commodity exposure because you believe we are in a secular bull market in energy, or believe that global growth will remain strong, the GSG will likely provide better leverage to those themes. Once again, it pays to think not just of the product in isolation, but also of how it relates to your overall portfolio.

For investors who are looking to gain a more concentrated exposure to a particular commodity, there are funds that focus on just one subsector of the commodity asset class. Over the past few years, several funds have been launched that can provide exposure to just energy, metals, or agricultural products. Beginning with energy-related funds there are several offerings for investors who would like to directly invest in energy. Many of the new funds actually trade in London, but there are a few that can be purchased over

U.S. exchanges. The United States Oil Fund LP (USO) is an actual ETF that tracks the spot price of West Texas Intermediate Light (the benchmark grade for U.S. crude oil). The fund gains the exposure to the commodity by investing in futures contracts tied to this product. The fund, with approximately $600 million in market cap, charges a 0.50 percent fee. A similar exposure can be gained through the iPath S&P SCCI Crude Oil Total Return Index ETN (OIL). This exchange traded note also tracks the performance of West Texas Intermediate Light, although it commands a higher fee of 0.75 percent. For investors looking for a U.S.-traded fund offering energy exposure beyond crude oil, there is the PowerShares DB Energy Fund (DBE), an ETF that tracks the Deutsche Bank Liquid Commodity Index–Optimum Yield Energy Excess Return Index. In addition to crude oil, this index will also include natural gas as well as gasoline and heating oil. While these other energy-related commodities normally have a high correlation to oil prices, they can diverge. In particular, oil tends to be more tied to geopolitical events. Natural gas prices in the United States tend to be driven by domestic considerations, such as U.S. inventories and the weather. Finally, even without movements in the underlying commodity, so-called light products (products refined from crude) can also diverge from crude oil based on conditions at U.S. refiners.

In the metals subcategory, there are nearly two dozen different exchange traded notes and funds focused on various metals; unfortunately, the vast majority of them trade outside the United States. For investors limited to U.S.-traded instruments, the major offerings are focused on gold, silver, and one instrument for base or industrial metals. On the gold side, there are several choices, including both exchange traded funds and exchange traded notes. State

Street offers the streetTRACKS Gold Trust (GLD). The price of this trust reflects the price of gold bullion, with roughly a one-tenth ratio. This is the largest of the instruments based on the price of gold, with nearly $10 billion under management. The product trades for a relatively inexpensive management fee of 0.40 percent. Other offerings focused on gold include the iShares COMEX Gold Trust (IAU) as well as the PowerShares DB Gold Fund (DGL), an exchange traded fund that tracks the Deutsche Bank Liquid Commodity Index–Optimum Yield Gold Excess Return Index. The fees on the products are 0.40 percent for the iShares and 0.50 percent for the PowerShares fund.

In addition to gold, silver is also represented in the United States with the iShares Silver Trust (SLV) as well as the PowerShares DB Silver (DBS). Both funds have an annual fee of 0.50 percent. While there are variations on how the underlying indices work, both should provide a reasonably close exposure to changes in silver prices. When looking at these products versus the gold funds, investors should consider that precious metals do not always move in tandem. In fact, while both commodities are considered precious metals their correlation has been lower than expected. Over the past thirty years, the correlation between the two commodities has been approximately 0.60. Over the same period, a dollar invested in gold is currently worth approximately $4.50 while a dollar invested in silver has grown to slightly less than $3.00.

This is not to suggest that gold is a better investment than silver, and that investors should focus on one metal to the exclusion of the other. There are several reasons why performance between the two could differ. Silver has industrial applications that can cause its price to fluctuate with economic activity. In contrast, gold has historically been prized as a store of value and has subsequently been affected by both inflation expectations and the strength of the dollar. In addition, because of its long history as a medium of exchange, gold prices often benefit from geopolitical turmoil. Both gold and silver qualify as precious metals, but their different characteristics can and do cause their prices to diverge. Investors wanting to gain exposure to precious metals may want to consider positions in both a gold and a silver fund. On the other hand, if an investor is specifically concerned about the long-term value of the dollar, then gold is probably the better hedge.

Finally, there is an ETF that is designed to specifically track the prospects of agricultural commodities, the PowerShares DB Agriculture Fund (DBA). This fund provides returns based on the Deutsche Bank Liquid Commodity Index–Optimum Yield Agriculture Excess Return Index. The index currently comprises an equally weighted basket of four agricultural commodities, with no livestock: corn, wheat, soybeans, and sugar.[10] As discussed in the beginning of the chapter, agricultural commodities tend to trade on different fundamentals from the rest of the group. While energy and metals, both precious and base, tend to be primarily influenced by both inflation and expected economic activity, agricultural goods are predominately affected by weather and other local factors. As a result, they tend to be a specialty subgroup, even within the broader commodity asset class. If you have particularly strong opinions about next season's wheat harvest or coffee production, this instrument can provide a relatively cheap, 0.75 percent expense ratio, along with exposure to these assets. On the other hand, assuming your forecasts on El Niño and crop production are no more accurate than anyone else's, you may want to consider a fund that offers a broader commodity basket.

Investing in commodities follows the same rules discussed throughout the book. Focus on the risk factors you want exposure to, and avoid taking overweight positions in things you know nothing about. From a long-term diversification benefit, investors should have a modest portion of their assets invested in commodities. For those particularly concerned about inflation, commodities offer a hedge against paper assets, stocks and bonds, which tend to suffer during periods of rising inflation. As with stocks and bonds, in the absence of specific insights stick to instruments that offer broad exposure to the asset class, and minimize your risks associated with any particular commodity.

As described in the beginning of the chapter, even the broader funds have some very concentrated risk. The DJP has a heavy weighting toward agricultural commodities, which may diminish its value as an inflation hedge (agricultural commodities and livestock could decline in price due to industry-specific factors, even as overall inflation was accelerating). The GSG is also extremely influenced by energy prices, particularly crude oil, which makes up almost 50 percent of the index. So while based on broad commodity indices, both funds have a fairly concentrated mix of commodities. The subgroup funds could be used to balance out those commodity-specific risks. Consider combining the metals and agricultural funds with the GSG to dilute the energy concentration. At the same time, an energy and gold fund could mitigate some of the heavy agricultural exposure of the DSP. The point is to use the instruments in combination to create the exposure you are looking for. As additional commodity funds become available, it should become progressively easier to incorporate a broad basket of commodities into your portfolio, and avoid any unintended risks associated with an overconcentration in a particular commodity.

Chapter 8

ETFS AND ALTERNATIVE
ASSET CLASSES

Thus far, we have focused on what could be considered traditional asset classes and traditional betas. Even commodities have grown in respectability this decade, and would now merit some consideration even within a relatively conservative portfolio. Ultimately, however, an investor's goal should be to assemble the most diversified asset mix possible. As diversification helps to improve risk-adjusted returns, finding exotic assets is not an indulgence, but actually prudent. The problem is that most assets have some leverage to the economy, monetary conditions, or other common factors that drive stock and bond prices. Even truly exotic assets, such as fine art, are somewhat influenced by economic conditions, as the potential pool of buyers for Old Master paintings is at least partly determined by economic conditions (think of how well a New York art auction would go if the market crashed and the pool of hedge fund managers was suddenly no longer bidding).

That said, even if assets have some relationship with common risk factors, how they react to those risk factors can be quite different. Commodities thrive under rising inflation, while higher prices only serve to diminish the value of bonds and many stocks. For this reason, looking for new asset classes, even if they do share some similarity with the more traditional choices, is a worthwhile endeavor. And while an ETF on Old Master paintings has yet to surface, there is an increasingly long list of funds catering to what I will refer to as exotic beta. These include everything from funds designed to mimic the performance of REIT indices, to ones that focus on particular company attributes, such as the number of patents a firm has obtained. While some of these are quite small, and the category is still largely in its infancy, its development is encouraging. It suggests that investors can look forward to investing in different types of risk factors, some of which were previously impossible to access.

REAL ESTATE FUNDS

One area in which ETFs are starting to branch out is real estate. Unfortunately, to date there is no way to directly invest in real estate through a fund, although the mechanism for doing so is not hard to imagine. In recent years futures contracts have been launched that are designed to mimic the performance of home-price indices. While these contracts are still in their early stage, and are not particularly liquid, as liquidity does grow they could provide the underlying exposure for a pure real-estate exchange traded fund. For now, investors looking to gain exposure to real estate must content themselves with the various REIT offerings. REIT funds invest in securities, which themselves invest in real estate. While they are technically considered equities in the financial sector, they tend to have a relatively low correlation with other financial stocks, as their characteristics and business model are very different from that of the typical financial firm. As a result, they tend to trade apart from other stocks, even financials. The financial sector is normally highly correlated with the rest of the equity market, but this is less the case for REITs. Over the past fifteen years, the financial sector has had a 0.80 correlation with equity returns, but the correlation drops to below 0.40 when looking at the REIT industry. While not a perfect proxy for real estate, REITs can be viewed as a rough proxy for gaining exposure, albeit indirectly, to that asset class.

As highlighted above, diversification is the primary justification for investing in many of the alternative asset classes. While some of these asset classes may have a compelling secular growth story, even for those that do not there is a rationale for devoting a small portion of your portfolio to assets that have a low correlation with stocks and bonds. Real estate, at least U.S. real estate, appears to fill this role. The OFHEO U.S. House Price Index, which tracks home prices in the United States based on data from Freddie Mac and Fannie Mae, indicates that house prices have had virtually no correlation with large-cap U.S. equities. Since 1975, based on quarterly data, the U.S. housing market has had a –0.03 correlation with stock prices— a level that is statistically insignificant. This may come as a surprise to most people, but over the past thirty-two years, home prices and stocks have frequently diverged for extended periods of time. This was true in the early and mid-1990s, when stock returns began to accelerate, yet home prices stagnated until the latter part of the decade. For the period between 2000 and 2003, while global stock markets were crashing, home prices were starting to take off.

The asynchronous relationship between stocks and home prices is not an anomaly. Home prices also appear to have a low correlation with other asset classes. When compared with commodities, home prices have a surprisingly low correlation of less than 0.20. As both commodities and real estate represent real physical assets, it is interesting that they have not shared a higher correlation over time. This suggests that even if investors have a commodity position in their portfolio there may be a diversifying benefit to adding a small real estate position as well. Finally, real estate also shares a virtually zero correlation with government bonds. Real estate benefits from falling interest rates, as does the bond market. However, a weakening economy, which often accompanies a drop in long-term rates, tends to be associated with deteriorating economic conditions. As economic weakness usually goes hand-in-hand with rising unemployment, it is less surprising that bonds and real estate tend to be disconnected in their cycles. Falling employment and income impede home purchases and hurt the demand for real estate. In addition, defaults also tend to rise as the economy deteriorates, providing an additional source of excess supply.

So, when compared with all of the major asset classes, real estate appears to offer some diversification benefit. Now, most individuals already gain their real estate exposure through their single largest asset, their house. Why add to that position, when it already occupies a significant, if not dominant position in most investors' total net worth? If you are already a home owner, with a large portion of your net worth in your home, adding to that position through a real estate security or fund may have a limited benefit and may even provide unnecessary concentration in a single asset class. However, there are circumstances where adding a real estate fund would be additive to a portfolio. Renters who do not like their local housing market may gain exposure to a generalized real estate beta through a fund. Also, individuals whose home equity is a low percentage of their overall wealth may add to their exposure. Finally, and we will discuss this more in the last chapter, a home owner who was nervous about overall real estate conditions, but was reluctant to move, could use a short position or put option on a real estate ETF to help neutralize some of his or her overall exposure to the housing market.

As investors cannot presently purchase a fund that invests directly in real estate, REITs offer a potential work-around and some of the same benefits. Over the past fifteen years REITs have had a 0.35 correlation with large-cap U.S. equities. Their correlation with other asset classes has been even lower. While REITs are rate sensitive, as interest rate levels affect home affordability the industry tends to have a low correlation with the U.S. bond market. Since 1992, the correlation between REITs and an index of U.S. bonds has been less than 0.10. Finally, as with physical real estate, the industry has an equally low correlation with commodities.

There are currently a number of funds that focus on different types of REITs. These include securities focused on broad indices as well as more specialized ones such as commercial or residential real estate. Funds in this category include ones from State Street, BGI, Vanguard, and ProShares. In terms of broad indices, offerings in this sector include:

- iShares FTSE NAREIT Real Estate 50 Index (FTY)
- Ultra Real Estate ProShares (URE)
- iShares Cohen & Steers Realty Majors Index Fund (ICF)
- Vanguard REIT ETF (VNQ)
- iShares Dow Jones U.S. Real Estate Index Fund (IYR)

As with other categories, the primary difference between the funds is the index composition. With the exception of the Ultra Real

Estate ProShares, the funds all generally charge a management fee in the neighborhood of 0.40 percent. The exception is the Vanguard VNQ, which has a 0.12 percent expense ratio. The main differences between the funds will be the different indices they are based on. The exception to this is the ProShares offering. This is a leveraged fund, in the sense that the returns to the holder will be a multiple of the performance of the underlying index. In the case of the Ultra Real Estate ProShares the return will be two times the Dow Jones U.S. Real Estate Index. We will spend more time in the final chapter discussing the merits of leveraged funds, but for now suffice it to say that investors who purchase this device are increasing their risk and exposure to the sector beyond what their capital commitment implies (note that the increased exposure comes at a cost, as the management fee for this fund is nearly 1 percent, twice the level of the nonleveraged funds).

In addition to the broad real estate funds, there are also sector-specific funds, as well as a few vehicles that provide exposure to REITs outside the United States. Sector-specific funds focus on REITs that invest in one part of the property market, such as commercial, residential, or retail real estate. Examples of this category are iShares FTSE NAREIT Industrial/Office Index Fund (FIO), iShares FTSE NAREIT Residential Index Fund (REZ), and the iShares FTSE NAREIT Retail Index Fund (RTL). As with other sector-specific funds, these products will have a narrower composition, with securities focused on one particular sector, such as office complexes. For an investor who wants to gain exposure to real estate, but is concerned about prices in the residential market, some of these funds offer an alternative by providing for a more concentrated exposure to other sectors in the market. Finally, for those investors looking to gain exposure to real estate markets outside the United States, there is the SPDR DJ Wilshire International Real Estate ETF (RWX). The fund tracks the performance of the Dow Jones Wilshire Ex-U.S. Real Estate Securities Index. The fund's current allocation includes an approximate 25 percent weight in Australia and Japan, 20 percent in the United Kingdom, and roughly 10 percent in Hong Kong and Canada. A similar offering, although considerably smaller in size, is the WisdomTree International Real Estate Fund (DRW), based on a proprietary international real estate index. The fund has a slightly different mix of assets, with more emphasis on Australia, as well as Singapore.

ALTERNATIVE INVESTING THROUGH ETFs

So far we have discussed the asset allocation choices in the context of particular categories: stocks, bonds, commodities, and real estate. The question remains, what other asset classes exist? Beyond the ones already mentioned, there is the growing area of so-called alternative asset classes. These would constitute exposure to assets such as hedge funds and private equity. Historically, these have been available primarily to wealthy individuals and institutional investors due to regulatory reasons. The primary appeal of these asset classes has been twofold: the prospect for unusually high returns coupled with traditionally low correlation to other assets. While private equity has continued to generate high returns, hedge funds, as an asset class, are no longer producing the stellar returns evidenced in the 1980s and 1990s. To a large extent, this deterioration in returns is likely tied to the proliferation of funds over the past decade. With estimates putting the number of funds at more than eight thousand, and with more than $1.5 trillion under management, we are now in a situation where a vast number of funds are chasing the same strategies.

Beyond the quest for stellar returns, the motivation to own alternative asset products is not dissimilar from owning commodities or real estate, namely the prospect of increased diversification. Hedge funds have traditionally marketed themselves as uncorrelated with market returns. This is because many of them utilize strategies characterized as market neutral, in that they are short a similar value to their long positions. These types of strategies should produce pure or portable alpha, which should theoretically be uncorrelated with market movements. While the reality has not always matched the theory, it is true that managers who maintain true market-neutral portfolios should see relatively low correlations with more traditional asset classes. The argument for private equity is similar. These funds, which invest in nonpublic companies, should also offer diversification benefits to the broader market.

Replicating hedge fund portfolios or private equity exposure in an exchange traded fund is significantly more challenging than reproducing stocks or bond index returns. Indices by definition are standardized. Their strategy is easy to replicate as the holdings are published. In some cases, the mechanism by which the indices are calculated is also published. Hedge funds, or other alternative investments, are harder to replicate because you are never quite sure what the managers are doing. To attempt to mimic an alternative asset, a sponsor must make some assumptions about the risk factors that strategy is leveraged to, and attempt to replicate those risk factors through other instruments. Despite the complexity of the task, numerous firms are trying to produce instruments that produce returns that mimic alternative assets. While we have yet to see an exchange traded fund mimicking hedge fund returns, there have been attempts in other parts of the alternative space. One example of a new fund in this category is the PowerShares Listed Private Equity Portfolio (PSP). The fund, which is still relatively small with less than $200 million under management, seeks to replicate an index of public companies that, in turn, own large positions in private ones. The fund matches an index, the Red Rocks Capital Listed Private Equity Index, that includes thirty U.S. publicly traded companies with direct investments in more than one thousand private businesses. The underlying index is rebalanced and reconstituted on a quarterly basis.[1] While the companies in the index are public, the fund provides indirect exposure to small, private companies through the portfolios of the companies held by the fund.

The problem with a fund such as this is similar to the challenge of using REITs to gain real estate exposure. As the product you are investing in does not actually represent the ultimate beta you are looking for, but is instead a proxy, you may not wind up with the exact exposure you want. In the case of the PSP, the underlying index is mostly composed of financial firms, with a small weighting to holding companies and Internet firms. As financials tend to have a particularly strong relationship with the broader equity market, it is not surprising that the correlation between the underlying index and the broader market is high. Over the past twelve years, there has been a better than 0.70 correlation between the returns on the Red Rocks Listed Private Equity Index and the S&P 500. So the diversification benefit is significantly reduced by the fact that the index used has a strong correlation with the broader, public equity market.

If diversification is not achieved, what about the second argument for private equity, namely higher returns? In the case of the

Red Rocks Listed Equity Index, returns have indeed been substantially higher since the mid-1990s (I'm using the underlying index rather than the actual ETF return as the latter has only been trading since late 2006). The private equity index has returned an average of approximately 2 percent a month since inception, versus less than 0.80 percent for large-cap U.S. equities. However, the volatility has also been substantially higher, roughly twice the monthly volatility of the broader market. So going back to our earlier discussion of risk and return, the private equity index basically represents a high beta bet on the market. This is actually what you see when you examine the monthly returns of the private equity index versus the S&P 500. Private equity has a beta of approximately 1.35 to the broader market. So in effect, private equity, as it is defined in this product, represents a leveraged beta bet on stocks. While raising the beta of your portfolio is perfectly legitimate based on your risk tolerance, there are cheaper ways to accomplish it. In this case, the PSP charges a management fee of 0.70 percent. It is worth pointing out that the return on the private equity index is not perfectly correlated with the broader market, and as the refrain goes, past performance is no guarantee of future returns. It is entirely possible that the two asset classes could increasingly diverge in the future. But for now, investors looking for alternative investments should make their decision in the context of the previous chapters. Does the instrument offer superior returns once risk is taken into account? Second, are those returns correlated with the other assets in your portfolio?

The major point of the above exercise is to encourage investors to investigate the characteristics of even the so-called alternative products. This segment of the exchange traded market is still in its early stages, with the PSP being one of the first funds focused on this space. That said, many investment banks are working on techniques to replicate hedge fund–like exposures in a systematic way. To do this, an analyst would need to decompose the returns on an index or indices of hedge funds into different parts, such as volatility, international exposure, and the like. Once that is done, baskets of securities can be created to mimic those returns, and theoretically produce a return stream that would replicate those of various types of hedge funds. It is reasonable to assume that this financial engineering will eventually find its way into the exchange traded fund market. As investors evaluate these alternative vehicles, it will be useful to keep in mind the issues discussed above. Does the instrument provide superior risk-adjusted returns, or does it have a unique beta that justifies its inclusion on the merits of diversification? A fund that fails both tests, no matter how impressive sounding the name, is just old-fashioned beta dressed up in a new guise.

Beyond the funds packaged under the alternative banner, a growing number of ETFs are based on ordinary equity securities, but assembled in a unique manner. These are similar to the thematic funds discussed in the previous chapter, only the themes are becoming increasingly esoteric. Over the past several years, the funds in this category have gone beyond focusing on dividends, value, and industry, into other categories that do not line up with traditional types of risk factors. Some of these are simply new takes on industry and sector aggregations, such as funds focusing on clean energy. But others have distinct characteristics that cut across traditional categories. One example of this latter type is a recent launch for a fund focused on patents.

Claymore Securities has filed with the Securities and Exchange Commission to launch an ETF on the American Stock Exchange.

The fund is designed to track the Ocean Tomo 300 Index, an index based on the Ocean Tomo 300 Patent Index. This particular index aims to identify companies that have the most valuable patents relative to their book value.[2] A fund of this nature will cut across the normal dimensions into which ETFs are typically aggregated. It would theoretically include both large and small companies, and value as well as growth. An aggregation by patents is also likely to cut across sector and industry definitions. Biotechnology, technology, energy, mining, telecom, and even financial services may be represented.

So, if a fund like this cannot be classified by its traditional beta exposure, what exactly are investors getting? Presumably, investors are gaining access to companies with a high growth rate. There is an implicit assumption that companies with lots of patents are innovators, and will enjoy better earnings growth than companies with fewer patents. What is interesting about an ETF based on this type of philosophy is that it actually brings the discussion of alpha and beta back full circle. In trying to discern characteristics associated with higher growth rates, the fund is actually following a similar goal to that of a fundamental analyst attempting to pick stocks. Perhaps patents do influence company performance. If so, this fund is looking to provide a glimmer of alpha under the cover of beta. And while one fund focused on a sole factor is not likely to constitute a renewed search for alpha, it is easy to see how combining a fund such as this with other like-minded funds lures a beta-focused investor back toward the search for alpha. A simple way to evaluate whether the fund is delivering would be to compare its performance to that of a growth fund. If the returns are similar, you may be simply getting growth stocks at a higher fee. Again, the question always comes back to the same issue. Does the fund add enough value to justify its fee, or are you simply getting beta dressed up to look like alpha?

The use of exchange traded funds as a vehicle for alpha is already being explored by a number of companies looking to launch the first actively managed ETFs. As of this writing, existing funds have been based on either an index or, like the HOLDRs, a set basket of stocks. But what if an exchange traded fund was allowed to take active positions different from the constituent weights of the index on which they are based? In that instance, you would ostensibly have a mutual fund that trades like a stock. The actively managed exchange traded fund is likely the next rung on the ETF evolutionary ladder, with several sponsors already working on such vehicles. Recently, Bear Stearns filed an application with the SEC to launch an actively managed ETF. The fund would invest in short-term fixed-income securities, mostly U.S. corporate debt.[3]

One of the main challenges with an actively managed exchange traded fund is the need for disclosure of positions. Existing index-based funds are fully transparent to investors, as their holdings are based on an index to which all investors have access. This creates the confidence to price the fund based on the holdings of the underlying instruments, and explains why exchange traded funds generally trade close to their net asset value. In contrast, active managers go to great lengths to obscure their holdings. While SEC regulations demand some transparency, this normally occurs with a significant lag, so investors are getting a glimpse into past, rather than current, holdings. Active managers are by definition taking bets on either proprietary information or analysis. Allowing other investors to see what they are doing dilutes the value of that information, and potentially lowers the returns associated with those strategies. So an actively managed ETF would need to balance disclosure requirements with the manager's need to maintain the intellectual property of the fund. In the case of the proposed Bear Stearns fund, the sponsor has opted for transparency, and has agreed to release holdings on a daily basis.[4]

Another example of the blending of active and passive management within an ETF are the funds sponsored by XTF, a New York–based money management firm. These funds, which trade for a relatively low 0.60 percent management fee, track long-term trends across asset classes to produce an optimal asset allocation for a given investor based on his or her risk tolerance. While the funds are not making active bets on individual securities, they are making tactical bets on asset allocation.[5] The sponsor actively adjusts the relative asset mix (i.e., stocks versus bonds) within the fund. The hope is to produce superior risk-adjusted returns over long periods, while still staying within the risk tolerance of a given investor. The firm has introduced a number of different funds based on this concept. The funds use models to determine the optimal mix of assets at the country or sector level. This is accomplished through a tactical asset allocation model that incorporates a number of fundamental, technical, and risk factors.[6] To some extent this is employing a different approach from one that tries to add value through stock picking. Nevertheless, its approach is still clearly active rather than passive. By changing the mix of assets in a tactical fashion, the sponsor is intending to add value through the judicious timing of markets, as opposed to simply mimicking an index.

As active exchange traded funds become a reality, investors will need to consider whether the same characteristics that make these funds attractive as beta extend to their search for alpha. When considering an active ETF, the decision should be no different from evaluating any other active manager. Whether based on subjective analysis or a quantitative model, can the manager add value after adjusting for incremental differences in risk exposure, and is that value high enough to compensate for the incremental rise in fees? In the case of the XTF funds the cost, 0.60 percent, is relatively low for an active manager. At the very least, a low cost structure presents a slightly lower barrier for success than most traditional mutual funds, which are often charging considerably higher fees.

As the market for funds grows, it is likely to continue to expand in diversity as well as size. While a sensible product, exchange traded funds are no more immune from the whims of fashion than anything else that is marketed. Sponsors will try to continually push the envelope and find the next new and exciting concept with which to entice investors. One example of this is the large number of recent fund launches focused on alternative energy and clean technologies. While this may be a perfectly legitimate investment theme for investors to consider, it is hard not to notice how its timing coincided with a growing awareness of global warming and weekly headlines on the merits of alternative energy.

As of this writing, there were 363 ETFs in registration.[7] Many of the new funds are simply slight variations on existing ones, funds that basically offer the same geographical or sector exposures, but use a slightly different index or weighting scheme. But included in the registrations and recent issues are some truly innovative funds. One example is Claymore BBD/High Income ETF (LVL), which was launched in late June of 2007. This fund tracks a proprietary index of 110 to 150 dividend-paying securities. What is unique about the fund is that the securities span multiple asset classes, including U.S. common stock, American depository receipts, REITs, master limited partnerships, closed-end funds, and preferred stocks. The fund, which charges a fee of 0.60 percent, is another good example of a nontraditional beta that represents a theme carried across different types of securities.[8]

Another example of an exchange traded fund pushing into the alternative space is the new iPath CBOE S&P 500 BuyWrite Index ETN (BWV). This is an exchange traded note based on the CBOE S&P 500 BuyWrite Index, or BXM. This note will mimic the performance of a combined long position in the S&P 500 overlaid with what is known as a covered call strategy.[9] A covered call strategy involves selling call options against your holdings to generate additional income (a call option is a derivative contract that allows an investor to profit from a rise in a stock's price, while a put option enables an investor to benefit from a drop in a stock's price). While not a full-blown options strategy, this product does manage to incorporate some of the more sophisticated options techniques into the return. In environments where options premiums are high (i.e., investors expect markets to be volatile), this strategy is likely to outperform a simpler long position in the S&P 500 index. The note, which trades on the American Stock Exchange, carries a 0.75 percent yearly fee.

The value of the more exotic funds is in their diversifying benefits (or theoretically in their alpha, should an active fund be able to demonstrate sustainable risk-adjusted returns above a benchmark). Exotic products always have their appeal, particularly when they are wrapped in the promise of stellar returns. Investors need to maintain a certain degree of skepticism in the "stellar return" part of that argument. Forecasting the long-term growth prospects of an industry is no less daunting than picking stocks or timing the bond market. In all three instances, you are making a tacit assumption that you have information or analytical prowess that the competition does not. Alternative energy may indeed wind up changing the world, but are you also able to accurately discount what these companies, most of whom have no earnings today, will be worth in twenty years? Many people were right when they assumed the Internet would change the world—it just did not imply that all the companies with a .com at the end of their logo would profit by it. Remember Pets.com and the sock puppet? When looking at exchange traded funds based on more exotic criteria, don't abandon the analytical framework that you would use on more prosaic instruments, like stock and bond funds. Does the beta diversify your existing portfolio, and what is the cost of obtaining that beta? As always, be skeptical on the alpha part.

Chapter 9

ADVANCED ETF TECHNIQUES

All of the previous chapters on exchange traded funds have assumed that the only choice for an investor was whether to own the security or not. But as discussed in the beginning of the book, there are other ways to exploit financial instruments, such as shorting a stock. In addition, there are also derivative instruments that allow you to take a leveraged bet, either positive or negative, on a given security or fund. In this final chapter, we will evaluate the arguments for considering these alternative strategies in an individual portfolio. Under what circumstances would an individual investor want to consider either going short or taking a leveraged bet?

All the methods and products discussed in this chapter will fall into one of two categories. The first category will focus on instruments and strategies that mimic what professionals refer to as leveraged or geared investments. These are strategies that either use leverage directly, for example buying an ETF on margin, or employ an ETF that represents a leveraged bet on an index. By leverage I am referring to any strategy where your return will be a multiple of the return on the underlying index the fund is tracking. Examples of these types of funds would include many of the new Ultra funds managed by ProShares Advisors. For example, an investor in the Ultra Russell 1000 Growth ProShares (UKF) would get a return of 200 percent of the Russell 1000 Growth Index. These funds offer the investor the opportunity to magnify his or her returns without the need to explicitly borrow money. Of course, if the index falls, losses are magnified as well. Beyond using margin accounts or funds with built-in leverage, there is another way investors can gain leverage in the ETF market: purchasing an option on an ETF. More and more exchange traded funds now have listed options. (An option is an instrument that gives you the right, but not the obligation, to buy another instrument at a set price. For example, an option on a stock would allow you to buy that stock at a certain price, say $50 a share, over a specified period, such as the next three months.) While the payout structure of an option is more complex than a simple multiple on a fund's return, the net effect is similar. These instruments represent a way to earn higher returns than would be possible with an outright purchase of an ETF.

The second group of strategies all entail, in one form or another, betting on a drop in price. The simplest way to do this is to short an ETF. We discussed the merits of shorting in the first part of this book. Shorting can be used to express a negative opinion of a security or fund. Including a certain amount of shorts within a portfolio can have the effect of improving the efficiency, that is, the risk-adjusted returns of one's portfolio. In addition to shorting, there are other ways in which an individual could express a negative view of an index or fund. ProShares Advisors, the same firm management company responsible for the leveraged funds, also manages funds that allow an investor to gain the inverse return. These funds would return the opposite of whatever the particular index or sector returned. So a short ProShare on the Russell 1000 would return 10 percent on the Russell 1000, assuming the index dropped by 10 percent. There are even UltraShort funds that allow an investor to take a leveraged negative bet. An investor who purchased the UltraShort Russell 1000 Growth (SFK) would obtain a return of 200 percent of the *inverse* of the performance of the index. Finally, in addition to shorting and funds designed to produce inverse returns, investors can also turn to the options market to benefit from an index's decline. Just as call options allow you to profit from a rise in a stock or index, put options provide the same benefit on the downside. However, investors need to be aware that, as with call options, put options also entail a leveraged bet. Investors who purchase a put on an ETF are likely to post large gains when the fund declines, but could lose their entire investment should the fund remain flat or appreciate.

BENEFITS AND RISKS OF LEVERAGE

While there are various ways to introduce leverage into a portfolio, does it make sense for most investors? While there are numerous choices, from purchasing call options to buying an ETF on margin (i.e., borrowing money from your broker to purchase a larger number of shares), are these techniques additive for most portfolios? In anwering this question, it is worth remembering that leverage raises risk. While you can obtain leverage in different forms, the net result is the same. Whether you borrow from a broker in a margin account or use options, all forms of leverage magnify the return on your investment. You will make more when you are right, and lose more when you are wrong. Using any form of leverage will always raise the risk on a portfolio. Going back to our definition of risk as the standard deviation of returns, risk rises as the returns become magnified. Leverage, in all its forms, will raise the return in positive months and lower the return in negative months. The net effect is that the absolute value of returns (whether positive or negative) will be bigger. Given the way that the standard deviation is mathematically calculated, this will raise the standard deviation, and therefore the risk.

However, what leverage does not do is change the risk-adjusted return (this is not entirely true, depending on how the leverage is financed, but stick with the simplifying assumption for now). As leverage raises return and risk, risk-adjusted returns remain constant. So leverage does not make you any smarter, just more aggressive. Now, if an investor has skill, and positive risk-adjusted returns, leverage will lead to higher positive returns, which is obviously a good thing. The degree of leverage that an investor employs then becomes a function of his or her risk tolerance. If you are willing to tolerate higher risk in the quest for higher returns, then leverage may serve a purpose. The key is to start off with an efficient portfolio, so that you are still producing the highest possible returns for a given level of risk, and only then employ leverage to raise the overall expected return on that portfolio.

As discussed above, if you want to add leverage to your portfolio, the traditional way—which applies to stocks as well as exchange traded funds—is simply to borrow money from your broker and purchase more stock or funds than you otherwise would be able to afford. In the case of a margin account, you are using borrowed funds to purchase additional stock. There are two implications of using margin. First, there is a cost. The broker charges you a rate of interest, called the call rate, to borrow the money. The call rate can vary over time, and is currently around 7 percent, although individual brokers may quote different rates for their particular margin accounts. For large accounts that trade frequently, the loan charged by the broker may be below the official call rate.

In addition to the cost of leverage, there is the increased risk. As an example, consider a simple portfolio that owns an interest in the SPDR S&P 500. If the SPDR traded at $100, an investor with $10,000 could purchase 100 shares, while an investor who borrowed the maximum amount allowed in a margin account, 50 percent, could purchase an additional 50 shares. Assume the cost of borrowing the extra shares is 5 percent, per year. If over the next year the SPDR appreciated by 20 percent, the first investor would earn $2,000 on his investment, or a 20 percent return. The second investor would do better. She owned 150 shares, which also appreciated by 20 percent, giving her a gross profit of $3,000. From that profit you need to subtract the cost of borrowing $5,000 to purchase the extra 50 shares. At 5 percent interest, the borrowing costs are $250. So the second investor made a net profit of $2,750 on her $10,000 investment, or a 27.5 percent return. Of course, if the S&P 500 dropped 20 percent, the second investor would also suffer a similarly greater loss. The use of margin increases the risk, in the same manner that owning a portfolio of high-beta stocks increases both the magnitude of the losses and the magnitude of the gains.

Thanks to the proliferation of new exchange traded funds, using a margin account is no longer the only way to magnify the returns on your portfolio. A new class of exchange traded funds can accomplish the same goal. The same net effect of a margin account can also be achieved by purchasing an ETF that incorporates leverage, such as the UltraShares. Either way the results are the same—the returns of an index are magnified—but in this instance the leverage is incorporated directly into the instrument rather than necessitating borrowing from the broker. There are two other differences between using a leveraged ETF and borrowing from the broker. First, the cost will differ. The cost of margin is a variable rate that will depend on the overall level of short-term interest rates. In contrast, the cost of a leveraged ETF is incorporated into the management fees, which tend to be significantly higher than unleveraged exchange traded funds. Which method is cheaper will depend on the instrument as well as the level of short-term rates. The higher interest rates are, the more likely a product like UltraShares will offer a cost benefit. There is another potential advantage of buying an ETF that incorporates leverage rather than borrowing using a margin account. If an investment goes against an investor, he or she may need to place additional cash in the margin account (i.e., sell other securities to make sure there is an adequate cash cushion in the account to cover any losses). In comparison, regardless of how a leveraged ETF trades, there is no need to adjust the cash in your brokerage account. Even if the trade goes against you, you already own the security. In other words, you did not need to borrow any money to purchase it. When a leveraged ETF posts a loss, you will lose money faster than with a normal ETF, but you will not receive a margin call, or request for more cash, from a broker. This does not stop the fund from posting significant losses, but the investor has no need to adjust his or her cash position in response to this. In this respect, an ETF with embedded leverage offers better flexibility than gaining the leverage through the use of margin.

There is a final technique that investors can employ to magnify the returns on their investment. Options enable an investor to commit a relatively small sum to an investment, with the prospect of earning higher returns. As with other investments that explicitly or implicitly use leverage, option investors can also lose money much more quickly, including their entire investment. For the purposes of this discussion, I will assume that an investor has a cursory understanding of the options markets. While whole books are dedicated to options trading and pricing, the key point for this chapter is that options are derivatives constructed to allow investors to take leveraged bets on securities or indices. Purchasing an option gives an investor the opportunity to buy or sell the underlying security or fund at a certain set price, called the *strike price,* before a certain date, after which the option expires and becomes worthless. Over the past several years, more and more exchange traded funds have developed a listed options market.

One of the biggest challenges of using options as a way to leverage returns is the transaction costs associated with the trading. For example, while a popular ETF like the SPDR commands a relatively liquid options market, with numerous expiration months and strike prices to choose from, other funds provide significantly less liquidity (options come with expirations denoted by a month and year, while the strike price is the price at which an option can be exercised). Say you are an investor who is particularly bullish on the telecom industry. One way to monetize that idea would be to purchase at- or out-of-the-money calls on an industry ETF. For a call option, if the strike price is the same as the current price, the call is considered at-the-money; if the strike price is above the current price, the call is considered out-of-the-money. The more the current price is below the strike price, or out-of-the-money, the more the theoretical purchaser stands to make if the stock rises significantly. The reason deep out-of-the-money calls make the most money when they pay off is that they are the most risky. The vast majority of the time, if you purchase a call with a strike price way above where the stock is trading, that option will normally expire worthless. Only very rarely will the stock appreciate enough so that the option has any value. As with everything else we have discussed, greater potential reward comes with enhanced risk. Out-of-the-money call options entail a greater likelihood that the investor will lose his or her entire investment.

Now, for an investor who wants to take a fling on the telecom space, the problem is not a lack of options for this sector, but the costs associated with employing the options. The costs are relatively high given that the options market for many of these funds is still developing. As a result, liquidity is still a work in progress. Several sector funds focus on telecom shares, including:

- iShares S&P Global Telecom (IXP)
- WisdomTree International Communications Sector Fund (DGG)
- Vanguard Telecommunications Services ETF (VOX)
- PowerShares Dynamic Telecommunications & Wireless Portfolio (PTE)
- iShares Dow Jones U.S. Telecommunications Sector Index Fund (IYZ)
- Telecom HOLDR (TTH)

So an investor has a number of choices. However, there are several complications. First, not all of these funds have publicly traded options. While the IXP, VOX, IYZ, and TTH all have options, the DGG and PTE do not. In addition, even for those funds that have listed options, there are likely to be limitations on the variation available. For example, it may be hard to find an actively traded option that lasts for more than a few months.

Even in those cases, such as the TTH and IYZ, that offer numerous choices as to the expiration date and strike price, transaction costs may become a significant issue. Because options, particularly those that are at- or out-of-the-money, trade for only a few dollars, wide spreads in between what you can buy it for—bid—and sell it for—ask—can have an enormous impact on the costs of trading. If an option trades for $2.00, but the spread between the bid and ask is $0.40, the transaction cost of the trade, before commissions, is 20 percent. That is a high hurdle rate to overcome, and represents a significant disadvantage to using options to attempt to gain leverage on your trades.

Finally, using options to gain leverage has an additional challenge not limited to options on exchange traded funds. Because options by nature are time dependent, or "wasting assets," an investor who uses options needs to get not only the direction right, but also the timing. If you purchase an out-of-the-money call option on a sector ETF in January with an April expiration, you are predicting that the sector will rise in price over the next four months. If the sector is flat during that time period, but starts to appreciate in June after the option expires, the option investment will produce a –100 percent return assuming the option is held to maturity. In contrast, an investor who utilized either a margin account or a leveraged ETF would not be under the same time constraint. The advantage of options is that they offer a greater amount of leverage than other mechanisms. For an investor or trader who is looking to produce triple-digit returns in sector, country, or style investing, options represent a degree of leverage that is unavailable through other instruments. The downside is that a wrong bet will cause you to lose your entire options investment.

To a large extent, the above discussion of options oversimplifies their uses, as there are numerous other trading strategies that can be employed. Many of these other techniques are less risky, and combine the buying and selling of different options with various expiration dates and strike prices. The techniques are beyond the scope of this book, but do merit one word of caution. If you are looking to use options to enhance the returns on your ETF portfolio, realize that these instruments introduce an entirely new layer of complexity and risk. Options are complicated instruments, whose value depends upon several factors besides the price of the stock. Time to expiration, interest rates, and the volatility of the underlying fund all affect the price an option trades at. For these reasons, options, whether on ETFs or single stocks, are not the ideal place to cut your investment teeth, and should probably be avoided by all but the truly sophisticated investor.

While options are the extreme sport of the investment world, leverage in general should be used with discretion and respect. There are legitimate uses of leverage, many of them having to do with how to efficiently allocate capital, but many of the methods that drive these uses are relatively sophisticated, and should come with the same warnings as stunts performed on television: don't try this at home. Investors who are looking to gain additional leverage in their portfolios should consider many of the leveraged funds, which can produce multiple returns. However, investors should also be aware of the fees associated with these products. While they are likely to prove cheaper than opening a margin account, the fees are normally a multiple of those charged for unleveraged versions of the same funds. An investor who uses these is not only raising the risk on his or her portfolio, but raising the transaction costs as well.

EXPRESSING NEGATIVE VIEWS THROUGH ETFs: SHORTING AND INVERSE FUNDS

While leverage typically expands the risks associated with an investment, shorting can paradoxically lower the risk as it can lead to more efficient portfolio construction. Professional fund managers refer to the inability to go short as the *long-only constraint.* If you were to combine different securities or funds into the type of optimization described in the first half of this book, one of the outputs of that optimization would be negative positions for some holdings. In other words, the combination of securities or funds that would produce the maximum return for a given level of risk would necessitate holding negative or short positions in some of those securities. By not being able to short securities, you are putting a constraint on your portfolio that will prevent you from obtaining the optimal risk-adjusted return. The extent to which this constraint hurts performance is a function of the assets in the portfolio. Generally speaking, an aggressive strategy involving a large number of low-volatility assets will benefit the most from the long-only constraint. The more aggressive, or risk seeking, a strategy, the more the long-only constraint will lead to a suboptimal portfolio, which does not maximize return for a given level of risk.[1]

The solution to this constraint is to loosen it, and permit a modest amount of shorting within the portfolio. Shorting will provide several benefits. First, it will make it easier for the portfolio to approach the optimal combination of assets. A second benefit will allow an investor to express a negative view on a segment of the market more effectively. Consider the example of a stock within an index. Most indices are highly concentrated, with the largest stocks making up the majority of the index, and the vast majority accounting for less than 1 percent of that index or market. Even if you had perfect foreknowledge that a stock was going to underperform, you would be limited in your ability to take advantage of that information unless the stock happened to make up a large portion of the index. This is because under the long-only constraint, the most negative position you could take on a security is to not own it. For most securities, the price of not owning them is trivial, as they account for such a small portion of the market. In contrast, if you can short a stock, you can fully express a negative view on it. If the stock drops 50 percent, you will gain 50 percent on your short sale (minus the associated costs surrounding the execution of the short). For this reason, shorting can be an effective tool in investors' portfolios, and one that tends to be underutilized by retail investors.

Within the exchange traded fund space, shorting can also bring benefits for the same reason. It will allow you to express a negative view on a segment of the market, as well as allow for more efficient portfolio construction. Think of a simple example where you want to be long on the U.S. market, but believed a segment of the market, technology, was overvalued. In order to construct a portfolio that fully implemented your views, you could buy nine separate sector funds and exclude technology. In addition to being cumbersome, this might also be more expensive, as the sector funds tend to have higher management expenses than the broader market funds. An alternative way of capturing this insight would be to buy a broad-based market fund, such as the S&P 500 SPDR, and then short a technology ETF to remove that exposure from the portfolio. This method has the additional advantage of better capturing your negative view on the tech sector. Under the first alternative, if you are right and technology is overvalued, you will not be hurt by its decline in price, but neither will you benefit from it. In contrast, under the second alternative, you would actually gain on any absolute price decline in technology shares. The risk is that if you are wrong, and short the tech sector when it rises, you will lose money on the position, where under the first scenario you would be unaffected by its performance.

As with gaining leverage, there are several ways to gain short exposure using exchange traded funds. The simplest and most direct way is to short the fund, just as you would short a stock. But in addition, there are also funds that are specifically designed to generate returns inverse to the performance of an index. Finally, investors can once again look to the options market to monetize negative information on a fund. Investors can use put options on exchange traded funds to directly benefit from the drop in a particular index.

Most exchange traded funds can be shorted. Shorting involves borrowing stock from a broker to sell, with the intention of buying the stock back later at a lower price. The largest issue on shorting an ETF will be the cost of borrowing. Lenders of stocks, mostly institutional investors, charge a fee to lend out their stocks to short sellers. Depending upon the relative popularity and liquidity of the security, the cost can be relatively small, upward to 3 or 4 percent or even more under certain market conditions. As a result, shorting a stock involves a significant cost. In addition, shorting also entails establishing a margin account.

As was the case with leverage, investors now have an alternative to using a margin account to short. Several ETFs are now based on what is known as an inverse index, in which they profit from an index's decline. Funds in this category include several sponsored by ProShares, including inverse funds on the Dow Industrials (DOG), S&P MidCap Index (MYY), NASDAQ 100 (PSQ), Russell 2000 (RWM), S&P 500 (SH), and S&P 600 Small Cap (SBB). In addition, ProShares has combined the concepts of contrarian with those of leverage and created funds that return a multiple of an inverse index. These funds are referred to as UltraShort ProShares and will return twice the inverse return on an index. Funds in this category include those on all the indices listed above. All of the funds trade with a 0.95 percent management fee.

The final method for gaining exposure to negative insights would be to use put options on listed exchange traded funds. Here the issues are similar to those involved with purchasing calls, specifically the diversity of options that are covered, the timing of the trades, and finally the transaction costs associated with implementation. For example, an investor who wanted to monetize a negative insight on the U.S. consumer discretionary sector would be able to purchase a put option on the Consumer Discretionary Select Sector SPDR Fund (XLY). However, on a recent trading day the at-the-money options were trading at approximately $0.60 per share, with a $0.10 spread. In other words, the spread cost alone would equal approximately 16 percent of the value of the option, a large threshold to overcome when gauging the potential profit. This challenge is on top of the previously mentioned issues concerning the necessity to time the trade accurately enough so that the sector sells off before the option expires.

The list of advanced strategies discussed is intentionally abbreviated, particularly the ones related to options. Overall, investors need to be increasingly wary as the strategies they employ grow in complexity. The availability of sophisticated products does not necessarily imply a universal competence to employ them. In this respect, financial products are similar to cars. A dealer will happily sell you a Ferrari, even if you've never driven anything other than a Taurus. A recent story in *The Wall Street Journal* highlighted Wall Street professionals buying $500,000 sports cars they had no experience driving. Many of these cars promptly wound up wrapped around highway dividers in Greenwich, Connecticut. Investors should treat leverage, particularly when it involves the complexities of options trading, with the same caution. Remember, many of the investment bankers who crashed their new Porsches into streetlamps made their money by selling high-priced products to investors who might have been better off without them.

While investors should adopt a cautionary attitude toward the leveraged flavors of exchange traded funds, there is more of an investment rationale for including some shorting or contrarian products in the portfolio. Not only does this allow an investor to express a negative view, but more important, most academic studies suggest that there are portfolio efficiency gains—better risk-adjusted returns—when some amount of shorting is included in the portfolio. That said, most studies suggest that most of the efficiency gains occur with a relatively modest amount of shorting, somewhere between 10 percent and 30 percent of the portfolio. Investors should be particularly cautious with those funds that offer a leveraged short bet. As with leverage on the long side, losses mount much more quickly when you are wrong. In general, most of the techniques and products in this chapter should be incorporated sparingly. It is not that there is no benefit or legitimate purpose to leverage or shorting, just that they need to be used judiciously and in the proper manner.

CONCLUSION

As highlighted in the first few chapters, investors should always remember that financial markets, and their participants, can be hard on the ill prepared and sloppy. Nothing about ETFs changes that truism. While a useful tool, they are just that, and only of use to the extent that an investor exercises careful judgment and a sound investment philosophy. Exchange traded funds are not a panacea for the challenges facing retail investors, nor do they bestow any marginal skill on the investor who utilizes them. Being able to efficiently purchase Malaysian equities or mortgage-backed securities does not make you any more adept at judging the relative merits of either investment. Both carry risks. And while those risks are somewhat different from the stock-specific risks discussed in chapter 2, it does not imply that country timing or industry selection are any easier to master.

Instead, the value of ETFs comes in removing a friction. As discussed throughout the book, diversity is an investor's one true friend. Other than skill, which, to paraphrase F. Scott Fitzgerald, is not parceled out equally at birth, diversity is the one characteristic that can enhance risk-adjusted returns. It does this not by guaranteeing higher returns, but by ensuring that the returns you do have are complementary to one another. The other benefit of exchange traded funds is that they are for the most part a relatively cheap mechanism for investing. And while there are certainly instances where a cheaper index fund may exist, as a broad investment choice, these instruments are one of the cheaper mechanisms for building individual portfolios.

As this book has been as much about how to invest, as what to invest in, it is worth summarizing the basic principles that individual investors should tape to their bathroom mirror. And while their implementation may differ, these basic principles are similar to those adopted by professional investors. The computer power and statistical tools of the quant may be beyond the reach of the larger public, but the principles driving those models are identical. All investors, not just the pros, can significantly improve their performance by asking three simple questions whenever they add a new asset to their portfolio.

1. Does the asset offer superior risk-adjusted returns?
2. How correlated, or related, are the returns of that asset to those of the other holdings in my portfolio?
3. What will it cost me in fees and transaction costs to access those returns?

The last question is the most obvious, although frequently ignored by investors. When evaluating costs, keep in mind *all* the costs, not only the up-front ones. For exchange traded funds that means the management or expense fees as well as the costs of buying and selling the funds. If, instead, you are contemplating investing in a more traditional mutual fund, make sure to include not only the management expense, but also administrative fees, plus any "loads" the fund may incur.

The first two questions are a bit harder to answer, but equally crucial to consider. If this book has accomplished nothing else, I hope it has at least gone some way in convincing you that returns, without the context of risk, are meaningless. Anyone can quote superior returns, particularly if they are creative with the time frame they use to measure those returns (e.g., including the three-year but not the ten-year track record). Even when a manager is not intentionally trying to mislead, it is impossible to know if the returns quoted are a function of risk or skill, if the risk around those returns is not part of the discussion. Studies consistently demonstrate that even successful managers are right only a fraction more than they are wrong. Despite assurances to the contrary, both luck and risk play a huge role in the investment outcome. When evaluating the success of that outcome, the exercise must focus on risk-adjusted returns, rather than just returns in isolation. If your risk appetite is such that you're comfortable increasing your risk in the search for higher returns, that is a perfectly rational and reasonable choice. Even more, for younger investors it is probably the correct choice. Nevertheless, separating out the risk from the return will prevent you from overpaying. Remember, skill is dear, but aggression comes cheap.

Finally—and this is perhaps where individual investors are in need of the most significant behavior modifications—don't make investment decisions in isolation. No matter how much you love or hate an individual stock or fund, the decision on what to buy and sell should not be made as an isolated choice, but should always consider the broader context of your overall portfolio. What does your portfolio look like with and without the stock in question? How does the inclusion of a fund or security change the risk profile of your portfolio? While it is harder to answer this question without the benefit of the various tools to which quants and other professionals have access, try to think of the issue in broad terms. Does one fund represent all of your small-cap exposure? Does the addition of a new fund add more exposure to commodities than you really want?

Investors should apply the same logic not only for funds or stocks they like, but also for those they don't. Even if you are not particularly bullish on commodities, maintaining a small position in this asset class has been shown to have a beneficial impact on most portfolios, as it creates a better-diversified asset mix. The same arguments hold for alternative asset classes as well, at least to the extent that you can find a financially efficient way of gaining exposure to them. In an arena where there are few easy answers or quick solutions, diversification is one of the most powerful tools available to investors.

Like most admonishments, the above list is easier to articulate than to follow. The problem with investing, like dieting or staying in shape, is that the right solutions are generally the more painful ones: sticking with a discipline even when it is not working, avoiding tempting fads, disavowing the fast solutions, and not always following the crowd. But adhering to the basic rules does work—not in the sense of producing overnight riches, but in the more realistic context of producing solid, long-term, inflation-adjusted returns. And to the extent that exchange traded funds allow you to better diversify and control risk at a cheaper cost, they are as close to a "quick fix" as you are likely to come by. ETFs will not necessarily make you a smarter investor, but they should make you a more efficient one, and as this book has gone to some length to point out, efficiency is an underrated virtue.

ACKNOWLEDGMENTS

This book would not have been possible without the support and encouragement of Barclays Global Investors. While not responsible for the content of the book, many individuals at BGI have been a key source of knowledge, as well as extraordinarily generous with their time and thoughts. I would like to particularly thank the management of the Active Equities team, Minder Cheng, Naozer Dadachanji, Ernie Chow, and Jonathan Howe, for providing an intellectually open and challenging environment, which facilitated the research and thought process behind the book. I would also like to acknowledge the iShares team, specifically Lee Kranefuss, James Polisson, Andrew Arenberg, Brad Pope, and Ira Shapiro, for their support and guidance. In addition to the many individuals at BGI, a number of other people have been critical in the preparation of this book, including David B. Stickney at Merrill Lynch, Eric Stubbs at Bear, Stearns & Co. Inc., and Kim Arthur at Main Management, LLC. Finally, I want to thank my wife Alice and son Palmer for being patient and understanding through many missed weekends and absent nights.

NOTES

INTRODUCTION

1. Deborah Fuhr, "Exchange Traded Funds: Year End 2006 Global Review," Morgan Stanley, February 22, 2007, p. 1.
2. Ibid.
3. Ibid.
4. Martin Leibowitz, "Alpha Hunters and Beta Grazers," *Financial Analysts Journal*, Sept.-Oct. 2005, p. 32.

CHAPTER 1: REALISTIC RETURNS

1. "A Case for Dividend Investing: Understanding the Historical Perspective—And Evolving Trends in Equity Markets," Legg Mason, 2007, accessed at investorservices.leggmason.com.
2. Robert J. Shiller, *Irrational Exuberance,* 2nd ed. (Princeton, N.J.: Princeton University Press, 2005), chapter 1.

CHAPTER 2: INCREASING SOPHISTICATION

1. Terrance Odean, "Do Investors Trade Too Much?", *American Economic Review* 89 (Dec. 1999): 1279–98.
2. Ibid.
3. Ibid.

4. Martin Leibowitz and Anthony Bova, "Alpha Returns and Active Extensions," Morgan Stanley Portfolio Strategy, Aug. 31, 2006, p. 2.

5. Brad M. Barber, Yi-Tsung Lee, Yu-Jane Liu, and Terrance Odean, "Do Individual Day Traders Make Money? Evidence from Taiwan," abstract, May 2004.

6. Alex Frew McMillian, "Timing When to Sell Stocks—It's important to have a sell strategy, but many trade too much too soon," money.cnn.com, Sept. 20, 1999.

7. Ibid.

8. The Conference Board, "U.S. Institutional Investors Continue to Boost Ownership of U.S. Corporations," Jan. 22, 2007.

9. Ibid.

10. Kevin Burke, "Not the Man, But the Machine," *Registered Rep,* Sept. 1, 2006.

11. "Quantitative Analysis of Investor Behavior," Dalbar Inc., July 2003.

12. Katherine Burton and Adam Levy, "Citadel Returns 26 Percent, Breaks Hedge Fund Mold, Sees IPO," Bloomberg.com, Apr. 29, 2005.

13. Luke Timmerman and David Heath, "Drug researchers leak secrets to Wall Street," *The Seattle Times,* Aug. 7, 2005.

14. "Law of Averages," *The Economist,* July 23, 2003.

15. Ibid.

16. "Why Index Funds Outperform Active Managers," Savant Capital Management, p. 5. www.savantcapital.com.

17. Ibid.

18. Ibid.

19. Ibid.

20. Ibid.

21. Adam Shell, "Hedge Fund Returns Could Be Misleading," *USA Today,* Nov. 21, 2004.

22. Mark Hulbert, "Strategies: A drag on hedge fund returns," *International Herald Tribune,* Mar. 9, 2007.

23. William Sharpe, "The Arithmetic of Active Management," *The Financial Analysts Journal* 47: 1 (Jan.-Feb. 1991): pp. 7–9.

24. "Why Index Funds Outperform Active Managers," Savant Capital Management, p. 3. www.savantcapital.com.

25. John Bogle, "Remarks Before the Center for Investors Education," Washington, D.C., Mar. 31, 2004.

26. "Why Index Funds Outperform Active Managers," Savant Capital Management, p. 3. www.savantcapital.com.

27. "Law of Averages," *The Economist,* July 23, 2003.

28. "Why Index Funds Outperform Active Managers," Savant Capital Management, p. 5. www.savantcapital.com.

CHAPTER 3: ALPHA AND BETA: SEPARATING SKILL FROM RISK

1. Richard C. Grinold and Ronald N. Kahn, *Active Portfolio Management,* 2nd ed. (New York: McGraw Hill, 2000), p. 36.

2. Ibid., pp. 16–17.

3. Ibid., p. 13.

4. Yannick Daniel CFA, Manish Singh, and Jean-Baptiste Mayer, "Portfolio Engineering—Decoupling alpha and beta with Exchange Traded Funds: the future of portfolio performance?" Société Générale/Cross Asset Research, Spring 2006, p. 6.

5. Ibid.

6. Grinold and Kahn, *Active Portfolio Management,* pp. 16–17.

7. Ibid.

8. Edwin Burmeister, Richard Roll, and Stephen A. Ross, "Using Macroeconomic Factors to Control Portfolio Risk," unpublished paper, Mar. 9, 2003.

9. Grinold and Kahn, *Active Portfolio Management,* p. 173.

10. Ibid., p. 55.

11. Martin L. Leibowitz, "Alpha Hunters and Beta Grazers," *Financial Analysts Journal,* Sept.-Oct. 2005.

CHAPTER 4: INTRODUCTION TO EXCHANGE TRADED FUNDS

1. Deborah Fuhr, "Exchange Traded Funds: Year End 2006 Global Review," Morgan Stanley, Feb. 22, 2007, p. 4.

2. Ibid.

3. Fuhr, "Exchange Traded Funds: Year End 2006 Global Review," p. 86.

4. Ibid.

5. ETF Connect, Nuveen Investments, etfconnect.com.

6. Fuhr, "Exchange Traded Funds: Year End 2006 Global Review," p. 86.

7. ETF Connect, Nuveen Investments, etfconnect.com.

8. Fuhr, "Exchange Traded Funds: Year End 2006 Global Review," p. 86.

9. Ibid.

10. "Revolution or Pollution?", *The Economist*, Apr. 21, 2007, p. 83.

11. Fuhr, "Exchange Traded Funds: Year End 2006 Global Review," p. 1.

12. Ibid.

13. Ibid.

14. Ibid., p. 3.

15. Ibid.

16. Actively Managed Exchange-Traded Funds, Securities and Exchange Commission 17 CFR Part 270 [Release No. IC-25258; File No. S7-20-01], RIN 3235-AI35 Actively Managed Exchange-Traded Funds.

17. Ibid.

18. Fuhr, "Exchange Traded Funds: Year End 2006 Global Review," p. 4.

19. Howard J. Atkinson with Donna Green, *The New Investment Frontier III: A Guide to Exchange Traded Funds for Canadians* (Toronto: Insomniac Press, 2005), p. 179.

20. Ibid.

21. Katie Benner, "ETFs: A user's guide," money.cnn.com, Feb. 8, 2007.

22. Ibid.

23. Etfconnect.com/education/fundamentals.

24. Jim Wiandt, "Lee Kranefuss Interview," Indexfunds.com, Sept. 25, 2000.

25. Dan Colloton, "Are ETFs Really More Tax-Efficient Than Mutual Funds?", Morningstar.com, Feb. 14, 2006.

26. Ibid.

27. Diya Gullapalli, "Why Hot Funds Are Tripping Up Some Investors: ETFs, Which Are Meant to Track Benchmarks, Increasingly Go Astray," *The Wall Street Journal*, Apr. 19, 2007, p. A1.

CHAPTER 5: EQUITY ETFS: SECTORS, COUNTRIES, AND STYLES

1. Herb Morgan, "SPY vs. RSP: Market Cap Versus Equal Weighted ETFs," seekingalpha.com/article/6096, posted Jan. 25, 2006.

2. Ibid.

3. Ibid.

4. "Strategy and Tactics in Style Investing; Part 1: Combining Growth and Value Stocks," Bernstein Global Wealth Management, bernstein.com, posted Dec. 3, 2004.

5. "Value vs. Glamour: A Study of the Indices," The Brandes Institute, brandes.com, pp. 1–2.

6. iShares.com/fund_info_detail.

7. Ibid.

8. Ibid.

9. "Asia's Role in the World Economy," *Finance & Development* 43:2 (June 2006), p. 2.

10. Dominic Wilson and Roopa Purushothaman, "Dreaming with BRICs: The Path to 2050," Goldman Sachs Global Economic Paper no. 99, October 1, 2003.

11. Ibid., p. 12.

CHAPTER 6: FIXED-INCOME FUNDS

1. "The Importance of Understanding Fixed Income Indexes: How are indexes different from each other? Why understand the differences?" Barclays Global Investors, 2007; available from alhambrapartners.com.

2. Ibid.

3. Ibid.

4. Ibid.

5. "Mechanics of TIPS and TIPS ETFs," iShares.com, Barclays Global Investors, 2004.

6. Ibid.

7. Ibid.

8. Ibid.

9. iShares.com.

CHAPTER 7: COMMODITY FUNDS

1. "iPath: Using Commodities to Diversify Your Portfolio," ipathetn.com, Barclays Global Investors, 2007, p. 2.

2. Frank Armstrong III, CFP, AIF, "Commodities as an Asset Class," investorsolutions.com, July 15, 2004.
3. "About iPath Exchange Traded Notes: Overview," ipathetn.com, p. 1.
4. Ibid., p. 7.
5. "iPath Dow Jones–AIG Commodity Index Total Return ETN," ipathetn .com.
6. Ibid.
7. Ibid.
8. "S&P GSCI™ Commodity-Indexed Trust: Daily Holdings," iShares.com.
9. Goldmansachs.com/gsci/, Table 1: S&P GSCI Components and Dollar Weights (%), June 12, 2007.
10. DBA Home Page, dbfunds.db.com/dba/index.aspx.

CHAPTER 8: ETFS AND ALTERNATIVE ASSET CLASSES

1. powershares.com/products.
2. Richard Beales, "Profiting from a very good idea, patently," *Financial Times,* Nov. 24, 2006.
3. Lawrence C. Strauss, "Active Management and ETFs," *Barron's,* Apr. 2, 2007, p. 41.
4. Ibid.
5. Saskia Scholtes, "Hands-on investor: The benefits of a good average," *Financial Times,* Mar. 23, 2007.
6. Ibid.
7. Tom Lydon, "ETF Pop Quiz," ETFtrends.com, July 13, 2007.
8. Matt Hougan, "Claymore's New High Income ETF: Markedly Different Than Its Peers," seekingalpha.com, July 2, 2007.
9. ipath.com/buywrite-etn.

CHAPTER 9: ADVANCED ETF TECHNIQUES

1. Richard C. Grinold and Ronald N. Kahn, *Active Portfolio Management,* 2nd ed. (New York: McGraw Hill, 2000), p. 421.

INDEX